HOW TO **MAKE MONEY** WITH **MySPACE**

D1538444

OTHER BOOKS BY DENNIS L. PRINCE

How to Sell Anything on eBay . . . and Make a Fortune!, 2/E

Unleashing the Power of eBay

How to Sell Anything on eBay . . . and Make a Fortune! Organizer

101 Ways to Boost Your Fortune on eBay

With Lynn Dralle

How to Sell Antiques and Collectibles on eBay . . . and Make a Fortune

With William M. Meyer

How to Sell Music, Collectibles, and Instruments on eBay . . . and Make a Fortune!

With Sarah Manongdo and Dan Joya

How to Buy Everything for Your Wedding on eBay . . . and Save a Fortune!

HOW TO **MAKE** **MONEY** WITH **MySPACE**

Reach Millions of Customers, Grow Your Business, and Find Your Fortune through Social Networking Sites

DENNIS L. PRINCE

New York   Chicago   San Francisco
Lisbon   London   Madrid   Mexico City   Milan
New Delhi   San Juan   Seoul   Singapore
Sydney   Toronto

The McGraw·Hill Companies

1 2 3 4 5 6 7 8 9 0   FGR/FGR   0 9 8

ISBN: 978-0-07-154467-2
MHID: 0-07-154467-4

How to Make Money with MySpace is no way authorized by, endorsed, or affiliated with MySpace or its subsidiaries. All references to MySpace and other trade-marked properties are used in accordance with the Fair Use Doctrine and are not meant to imply that this book is a MySpace product for advertising or other commercial purposes.

Readers should know that online businesses have risks. Readers who participate in online business do so at their own risk. The author and publisher of this book cannot guarantee financial success and therefore disclaim any liability, loss, or risk sustained, either directly or indirectly, as a result of using the information given in this book.

McGraw-Hill books are available at special quantity discounts to use as premiums and sales promotions, or for use in corporate training programs. For more infor-mation, please write to the Director of Special Sales, Professional Publishing, McGraw-Hill, Two Penn Plaza, New York, NY 10121-2298. Or contact your local bookstore.

CONTENTS

ACKNOWLEDGMENTS

Here comes another great book made possible by the same great team that has made my work so much easier.

At McGraw-Hill, I applaud my project editor, Donya Dickerson, for much of the creative insight and enthusiasm. You're indispensable, incredibly motivating, and absolutely uplifting.

Also, I extend an equal vote of thanks to the rest of the terrific McGraw-Hill team with whom I've worked: Pattie Amoroso, Tama Harris, Anthony Landi, Seth Morris, and all the fine folks who serve as the creative and inspirational heart of the McGraw-Hill editorial/production, sales, and marketing teams. Thanks to each of you.

Next, my thanks to Roberta Mantis for the excellent copyedit. Thanks for your astute observations and suggested adjustments that have resulted in a much better text.

And, of course, I would be remiss if I didn't extend thanks to all the folks I've interacted with at MySpace. The pages you maintain are excellent, and the manner in which you've harnessed the site for business endeavors is admirable. I'll be wishing you all the best of success as your MySpace journey continues.

INTRODUCTION

In a casual chat with a friend the other day, I noted that it seems as though the Internet has been around for ever—in reality, it's been satisfying our needs and notions only since 1994. Granted, the "Internet" has been around for much longer, if you insist upon tracing back to 1969 and the original ARPANET effort mounted by the U.S. military. For practical purposes, though, the rest of us found the Internet midway through the 1990s, and it has changed the way we work, research, shop, and entertain ourselves. But, fueled by an incredibly quick adoption rate by the "regular folks" around the globe, plus the proliferation of better and more affordable hardware goods and gadgets, the Internet permeates our day-to-day lives in much the same way as the air we breathe.

What's the point? Simply put, the Internet has defined a certain portion of our selves as we've learned to tame it for our own purposes—as a learning tool, a communication method, and a means to financial gain.

Wait! This is a book about MySpace.com, isn't it?

Yes, it is and, as you'll quickly learn, it's about so much more. Just as the Internet has become integral to our lifestyles, it has also become pivotal in our livelihoods. Recall the dot-com boom of the late 1990s, the subsequent leveling off, and the eventual recovery. Millions of people worldwide have survived the early days and have successfully harnessed the Internet and its boundless access to start a business, expand an existing business, and essentially redefine how, when, and where business gets done. And while you might have considered MySpace.com to be anything but a business tool—just another of those online distractions where regular (and some not-so-regular) folks just like to virtually "hang out" and shoot the breeze—the truth is that it works remarkably well to proliferate thoughts, ideas, and aspirations, many of them linked to making money! That's right. MySpace can make you money. Interested?

WORD-OF-MOUTH MARKETING FOR THE TWENTY-FIRST CENTURY

"Social networking"—that's millennial terminology for the time-tested method of effective marketing—*getting the word out*. Word of mouth is still one of the best ways to increase awareness of a business and, thereby, increase a customer base. Why? Simply put, what better form or referral can you get than testimony from a trusted friend? Whether friends tell you about a great new movie, a hot new song, or the excellent product they just purchased, your friends often influence what you do, what you buy, and where you'll find it. And, when folks are hanging out at MySpace or any other popular social networking site, they're largely talking about these very things. It's word-of-mouth marketing running at the speed of the Internet, and it's no longer limited by any sort of advertising budget.

Now, despite some of the salacious exposés you might have seen or read, MySpace *is* a viable approach to direct marketing that allows you to reach literally millions of people of all age groups (especially the very difficult-to-attract teen population) at virtually no cost. Rather than attempt the old-fashioned and costly method of printing up direct mail literature or risk being targeted as a spammer for direct email distributions, MySpace allows you to establish your presence, be seen by an initial few visitors, and then let the community "buzz" do the rest. And if you wonder whether this social networking can really make an impact on business exposure and the bottom line, just take a look at how MySpace has attracted big players like Aquafina, HBO, Toyota, and even Disney.

MySPACE AND *YOUR* BUSINESS SUCCESS

The only problem with exciting new venues like MySpace is finding *your* way in to reap the benefits for yourself and your business. That's where this book comes in—it's the one resource you need to get in, get live, and get the most of MySpace's profit-enhancing potential. There's nothing new about online merchandising—perhaps you're actively mining the online marketplaces at eBay, Amazon, Yahoo!, or a Web site of your own—but online business-people know and agree that achieving a high level of Web exposure is difficult and often daunting. With MySpace, spreading the word about your business is practically effortless because, once your space is live, *the community does the marketing for you!* Thanks to the online phenomenon of social networking, you'll see your business's MySpace attract "friends"—folks who share a similar affinity for your interests, personal or professional—and who will eagerly add your space to their profiles, ultimately passing along the word to their network of friends and the friends of those friends, and so on and so on. You get the idea—establishing market exposure like that via traditional methods could cost you a fortune and take years to accomplish. Again, at MySpace, you can promote yourself and your business rapidly and rampantly in a matter of mere weeks.

Oh, and it's fun, too!

WHAT YOU'LL FIND IN THIS BOOK

If you've even heard of MySpace—and it's difficult not to have—then you'll know how active a portal it is, and you'll want to know how this book can help you join in and get the word out about your business or byline. Here's what you'll find within these pages:

Part 1: Understanding MySpace

Since it's expected that you're new to the MySpace phenomenon—or at least new to how to leverage it for your financial benefit—then this first part offers a requisite background to the site, its purpose, and its impact in the ever-expanding Internet experience. Here you'll gain the key insight that will help you find the best approach to the MySpace community, understand what succeeds and what fails within its virtual realm, learn the site rules and regulations, and develop your own plan to effectively enter the MySpace world.

Part 2: Establishing Your MySpace Presence

Next, you'll roll up your sleeves and begin developing your own MySpace page (or pages, as your plan may dictate). From registration to inputting initial content to applying more sophisticated design elements, this section gets your MySpace presence started up and moving forward. You'll not only learn how to utilize pictures, text, and nifty design elements but also how to make your MySpace page come alive with fresh content and interactivity that will draw more "friends" into the fold to help get the word out about you and your business.

Part 3: Look and Learn—Case Studies of Successful MySpace Marketers

When you're running a business, you're always looking for the fast track to success. That said, it makes good sense to study what your peers—and competitors—are up to and to what level of success they have achieved. Therefore, this part of the book takes a close look at 11 compelling case studies, other individuals and businesses that have turned to MySpace to boost their results and improve their business's bottom line. These are real stories from real going concerns that will fascinate you and further impress upon you the elements that work best to get the most for your business from a MySpace presence.

Part 4: More Ideas for Marketing *Your* Space

To wrap things up, this section takes a look at logical next steps for your MySpace endeavors to further proliferate your presence and profits. From ensuring that your space remains active in attracting new and repeat visitors to determining how MySpace works in conjunction with another Web presence you may have (or should consider establishing), this section points you in the direction of additional opportunity.

WHAT'S NOT IN THIS BOOK

Since this is a business-themed book, don't expect to delve into a tome of high-tech tools and tactics that will make you a MySpace wizard. The focus here is on how to angle a MySpace presence to benefit your business and, as you will soon read, often less is more when it comes to marketing online. If you are interested in digging deep into the spaces where the technical geniuses converge, you'll find some pointers to additional references—online and offline—to satisfy your curiosity.

The point of this book, then, is to get you knowledgeable and comfortable with MySpace so that you can establish your presence as quickly as is practical. Time is money and, well, you know the rest.

THIS SPACE AVAILABLE

Naturally, the Internet and its various portals and places are continually evolving. Therefore, expect that some things might change a bit at the MySpace destination, new tools will emerge and new regulations might arise. With this in mind, this book is written to be as change-proof as possible, again focusing on good business approaches that remain relevant despite technical modifications. Of course, this *could* affect how you apply some of the techniques discussed herein, and if ever you find yourself with additional questions, please don't hesitate to drop me a line and inquire. This book will continue to serve you well despite most site modifications, but if ever you find that you've reached a slowing point and want to chat further about applying the principles presented here, please contact me at dlprince@bigfoot.com.

For now, turn the page and begin to understand how MySpace can help you socialize your efforts and business aspirations, helping you find a larger audience and serve it in a way that will have its members chatting up your offerings 24 hours a day.

Let's get started.

UNDERSTANDING
MySPACE

WHY **MySPACE** MATTERS

Sure, this chapter's title seems like a loaded statement, one that could take this discussion in several different directions. For the purpose of this book and its intent, though, the focus will be on why MySpace matters to your business. Building a business and making money are very *communal* endeavors; that is, you'll need to attract a community to fully promote your wares or services, and you'll want to delight those who drop by so they'll let others know of the satisfaction that awaits them, too. To that end, this chapter looks at MySpace, what it is and how it became the most popular destination on the Internet (even outpacing the heavily trafficked Google). As you're readying yourself to include MySpace in your overall business plan, you'll find that you'll be best served if you understand what it is and what caused it to "tip" into rampant popularity, thus enabling you to apply some of that same magic to your money-making pursuits.

A NEW SPACE CALLED MySPACE

Although it's been the "darling" of its ilk, MySpace.com wasn't the first "social networking" destination online. Back in 1995— veritable *prehistoric* times for the Internet—Randy Conrads established Classmates.com (www.classmates.com) as a place where people could utilize the reach of the World Wide Web to discover where in the world their school friends wound up. The site was remarkably bland in its earliest days, yet it caught on and became a profitable venture as of 2001, buoyed by subscription fees and affiliate compensations. And while the endeavor seemed about as woefully nostalgic as thumbing through a decades-old yearbook and wistfully wondering where the years had gone, it has succeeded in attracting 40 million active members who reconnect via e-mail and plan reunion events. MySpace, of course, would take this concept of "personal places online" and expand it nearly five-fold. (See Figure 1.1.)

In November 2003, MySpace.com (www.myspace.com) was officially founded by Tom Anderson (currently serving as president of the site) (see Figure. 1.2) and Chris DeWolfe (currently serving as CEO). Previously owned by Intermix Media, a Los Angeles–based Internet marketing company, it was purchased by Rupert Murdoch's News Corporation in July 2005 for $580 million.

Figure 1.1 Noted as the first "social networking site" on the WWW, Classmates.com set the stage for MySpace.com when it introduced the concept of reaching out to friends, past and present.

MySpace Tip

Although I touch base on a few of the more *infamous* aspects of MySpace—and you're certainly aware of some of them as we begin this journey—don't expect deep dissertations on the darker side of the site. I'll look at some of the negative aspects of the site only to the point at which you'll want to take steps to shield your space from potential troubles along the way.

MySpace became a near-immediate hit online since it sought to provide a no-fee service to regular people looking for a way to

Figure 1.2 Have you seen this man? If not yet, you soon will. It's MySpace president Tom Anderson, and he'll be your first official "friend" when you register at MySpace.

connect with others having similar likes, dislikes, and just about anything in between. The site offered a no-frills method to establish an online presence and then encouraged the inviting of "friends" to join a space. Their friends, of course, would invite other friends, and away you go to establishing a network of friends and friends of friends and friends of friends of friends—you get the idea. (See Figure 1.3.)

MySpace got its biggest initial boost by catering to musicians—professional as well as amateur—by providing a means to upload music files that would feature new songs from an existing band eager to reach a larger audience or from new bands eager to just get listened to. It was a stroke of genius, really, given that the musical experience relies heavily upon the connection artists can make with their fans and the appreciation of fans for the artists who make themselves accessible. Therefore, the MySpace profiles that would be set up by page owners would allow uploads of images and multimedia files and would even support the posting of blogs, all designed to keep the content fresh and the friends coming back. It worked, and by 2004 the site boasted an impressive

Figure 1.3 MySpace.com is the place to be if you want to tap the power of a sizable social network.

1.5 million strong membership. Two years later, that number would increase amazingly to 70 million registered members and, as of 2007, the "community" is thriving with over 150 million active "Spacers."

So does meteoric growth like this signal that MySpace is just a fad and not likely to have any lasting value after the buzz dies down a bit? Not necessarily. There's a striking similarity between the rampant growth of MySpace and that of eBay (www.ebay.com) some years ago. In case you missed it, eBay, too, was founded with a small user community that converged to buy and sell just about anything in the exciting online auction format. The site's user base grew quickly, and the founder, Pierre Omidyar, and his partners sought someone with strong business acumen to run it like a serious business. As the site evolved and the community grew, many of the "old timers" complained that it was too big and it likely couldn't succeed as it had in its earlier days. Truth be told, eBay is still running strong and has proven to be a key ingredient in many business's marketing model. MySpace, incidentally, is positioned to do the same.

Although MySpace was buffeted by the participation of young people attracted to the emerging music scene within its realm, others who watched the site grow and mature saw that the young crowd had other "needs" to be met—fashion, food, fun, and so on. That's when brick-and-mortar establishments, from music stores to coffee shops and more, began to establish a presence at MySpace to let the community know where to get a new band's CD and where to stop off for some fresh java and complimentary wireless access in their local area. Essentially, these onlookers saw how the virtual "mall" where the Spacers were hanging out was still lacking in serving the rest of the community's needs; they wisely sought to correct that and collect on the effort. That's not exploitation of any sort—it's doing the good business of catering to the community.

MySpace Tip

You'll read more about some of these wise onlookers—folks who saw the potential of the MySpace community and the ways it could help spread the word about their business—later in this book.

GETTING TO KNOW THE
MySPACE COMMUNITY

Just like any business endeavor done right, you'll need to under-stand how your product or service will suit a community and then set up shop in a location and with a style that will attract your target audience. Just as brick-and-mortar stores are erected only after careful demographic studies, you'll likewise need to conduct a similar analysis to ensure that your MySpace presence will "stick" with the community, in whole or in part (that is, identifying a particular niche of the MySpace user base and aiming for their spe-cific attention). While the discussion of planning for the commu-nity is addressed in Chapter 2, take this moment to see who makes up the MySpace population as preparation for your business plan to come.

MySpace by the Numbers

It's not just curiosity that has driven many firms and concerns to closely study the MySpace *makeup*—the complexion of the com-munity as made up of different sorts of people from similar and differing points of view—but, rather, it's the desire to learn how to capture and possibly repeat the "lightning in a bottle" that is the MySpace phenomenon. The growth rate of MySpace, as previously stated, has been practically unheralded, yet it has caused such a stir in New Millennium demographics and economics that it has had the brightest minds buzzing to pin it down and dissect it to see what makes it tick. Leading online tally master comScore Media Metrix found MySpace to be genuinely diversified, age wise, as show in Figure 1.4.

Again, these statistics are key to a business approach; you will later determine the best approach to use—including MySpace

MySpace Demographics, October 2006

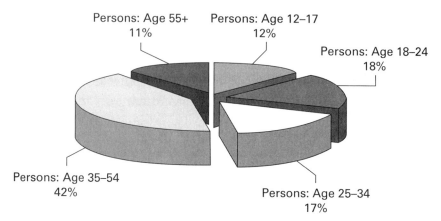

Figure 1.4 Recent numbers show how the MySpace community tallies up when weighing the age makeup of the massive user base. Source: comScore Media Metrix Press Release, October 5, 2006.

page design, content, and language—to attract the appropriate community segments (and the more crossover appeal you can generate, the better).

MySpace Tip

Interestingly, an October 2006 study by comScore Media Metrix (www.comscore.com) saw a trend in the MySpace demographic that indicated it was becoming more popular with older Internet users, those who maintain an active camaraderie with the younger contingent. Compared with a year earlier, the percentage of persons aged 25 to 34 increased by nearly six points, while the percentage of persons aged 35 to 54 climbed by eight points. Not only does this prove that the proverbial dog is never too old to hunt but also that there is a desirable diversity within the MySpace community, presumably driven by increased consumer power of the noted age groups, that all but ensures that you'll find an audience for your offerings.

So, if you had begun reading this book with a preconceived notion that MySpace is "kid stuff," it's not.

THE ABCs OF X AND Y

In the late 1960s and early 1970s, many of the up-and-coming young people complained about the stifling generation gap, that cultural divide that stalled and at best stilted communication between young adults and their elders, be those parents or authority figures. Actually, a generation gap can occur between any set of generations, and today we are beset with some interesting challenges between those in established financial lifestyles and those younger ones who may appear largely uninterested, proclaiming everything to be "lame." The fact is that all generations alive today are largely active consumers at heart, and all seek some sort of indulgence that provides pleasure and distraction of one sort or another. But to understand what each of the current generations seems to value, you first have to recognize the key generations segments themselves.

The Original Baby Boomers

Born between 1946 and 1964 and largely occupying the *age 35 to 55+* demographic segment, the Baby Boomers have been named the generation that put capitalism into full swing, some say driven by the fact that this was the generation to have been raised on television. The proliferation of television and national broadcasts developed like-mindedness among this generation. They viewed the same programming and were pitched the same products and services during commercial breaks. Likewise, music played a major role in developing the character and characteristics of Boomers; they toted newly acquired transistor radios to listen to the latest rock and soul tunes from the likes of The Beatles, The

Who, Jefferson Airplane, and the numerous artists responsible for launching the Motown Sound. Many Boomers are nostalgic these days, citing a lack of quality in current culture contributions— just like their elders did, right?

Generation X

Largely made up of the *age 25 to 34* slice of the community, members of this generation have the dubious distinction of being regarded as "slackers" mainly because of their attitudes of pessimism toward the future and skepticism and mistrust of traditional values (those of the Baby Boomers and prior). Whether you buy into that disparaging label or not, this generation nevertheless had its key influence on popular culture during the 1980s with respect to music, film, and television. From the advent of *grunge* music (with band Nirvana being most iconic in this movement) to the emergence of computer-generated film works, members of this generation have seen significant change in the social order that surrounded them, marked most significantly by the end of the Cold War and uncertainties of the domestic job market. While this generation was initially considered disenchanted with the Baby Boomers' financial values, the fact is that this generation ultimately grew up and became regarded as the upwardly mobile "twenty-somethings." This generation, incidentally, has entered into its own nostalgic realm and often refers to the 1980s and the early 1990s as the old days. In addition, this generation has well established purchasing power, largely dispelling the former tag of "slacker."

The Millennials

Don't call people in this group "Generation Y." This group resides in the *age 18 to 24* segment and is adamant about distancing themselves from any connection to the maligned Generation X. Instead, members of this demographic have deemed themselves the

Millennials because they emerged during the turn of the millennium and aren't quite as sullen or surly as their predecessors. Although many witnessed and can recall such devastating events as the Columbine shootings and the attacks of September 11, this is also the generation that experienced the boom of the personal computer starting in the mid-1990s. Members were old enough to grasp a mouse and poke at a keyboard as the millennium was readying to turn. But since the personal computer wasn't yet prolific during this generation's childhood years, they took to skateboarding (crowning Tony Hawk as their particular icon), hip hop music, and a piqued curiosity about something called a "Y2K bug."

The Internet Generation

And here comes today's pre-18-year-old segment, a generation that has been ushered fully into the Digital Age where personal computers, cell/camera phones, and downloads are prevalent. Members of this group will look quizzically at a vinyl LP or cassette tape, they'll mock any gaming system that came before Nintendo's Gamecube or Sony's Playstation, and they'll wonder why Grandpa's television has something called a "picture tube." This is the generation of immediacy and of abundant choice. Yet it's to be determined how they will emerge as young adults when it's their turn to take up the economic torch. In the meantime, they're all about MP3 players, video on demand, instant messaging, and highly caffeinated power drinks. This is the most difficult demographic to attract in any sort of measure of product or brand loyalty.

MySpace Tip

Although I won't continue on with this analysis of the various generations' monikers and makeup— fascinating though it is as a point of cultural study, not to mention tantamount to finely honing a business plan that accounts for marked shifts in consumer attitudes— I heartily recommend that you review the works of William Strauss and Neil Howe. These authors have made it their task to unravel and understand the history of American generations to excellent effect.

Of course, MySpace is driven by a community that develops its own online content and, therefore, controls what it will consume with a determination not afforded to Baby Boomers who were raised in a world of limited selection (they'll tell you about the days when there were only three major TV stations plus a handful of UHF independents). Don't take this lightly because the immediacy this community is accustomed to is difficult to pace or penetrate, forcing entrepreneurial types like you to either scramble to keep up with their changing desires or to effectively establish a niche that *you'll control and which they'll energetically seek out* (this last statement has been italicized since it is the "Nirvana" of a MySpace marketer).

BANKING ON YOUR REPUTATION

So with the discussion started regarding the MySpace community, take a moment to wonder how you'll emerge in this realm. That is, you'll want to begin to determine what sort of persona your presence will represent and what sort of reputation you might strive to develop within the community. When you decide to open your own space, then, you'll want to have considered how you'll initially present yourself and how that first impression will hook visitors.

Therefore, before getting into the actual planning steps that are covered in Chapter 2, for now simply browse around MySpace and look for other community members who may have similar interests or intent as you. (See Figure 1.5.) See which spaces compel you and which repel you. Surf the different pages to see how the community is flocking to pages that might be similar to what you'll

Figure 1.5 From the MySpace home page at www.myspace.com, enter some key search words that will help you find existing spaces that may cater to community members whom you hope to attract and entertain.

launch, and take notes about what commands your attention and would make you curious enough to want to pay repeat visits.

Let your noodle stew over all this, and let your imagination run wild a bit. Then apply a bit of business acumen that you may already have to ensure you can effectively "herd the cats" and to make sure that your approach won't be unwieldy and out of control. Mull this all over as you traverse the different pages you'll view and get ready to begin your planning for *your* space.

PLANNING FOR MySPACE IN YOUR BUSINESS

While I won't turn this discussion of creating a plan into a drawn out dissertation on business principles and market penetration factoids, it's nonetheless important to determine just *how* you intend to harness MySpace to further your business goals. If you intend to associate your MySpace presence with a new or existing business, you need to be sure that this presence is well represented and not undermined by your MySpace identity (don't be like those schoolteachers who never dreamed that their MySpace postings would ever be tied back to their professional lives; they were!). So this chapter briefly looks at things to consider as you ready your MySpace adventure and ways to make your start-up efforts go as far as possible. While a MySpace presence is an evolutionary process—you'll be tinkering with it continually, if you're smart—it's still a good idea to know where you'll start before registration day.

DETERMINING YOUR MySPACE APPROACH

There are no rules set is stone that deem it *required* you have a plan of attack as you register and construct your initial MySpace presence. In fact, there's a certain value in "winging it" to get a feel for the site from its barest sense and building from there. That's all fine and dandy, but you shouldn't expect to gain much traffic or requests to add friends if your space is made up of bare walls and a few sparse profile notes. Recall the browsing of the different MySpace pages you did at the end of Chapter 1. Then choose a space or two that you find to be revealing of good and not-so-good ways to construct a page. Now, look at Figure 2.1 to see an example we work from in this discussion.

Although a closer look is given to the DVD Verdict page later in Part 3 of this book, it makes for a good example of how to begin plotting a presence that can be as complete in a very short time. DVD Verdict maintains a buzzing Web site at www.dvdverdict.com and employs a "courtroom" of DVD "judges" who will screen new discs being released, giving court attendees a full debriefing on a disc's film content, technical merits, and overall innocence or guilt in hallowed halls of home entertainment. The site wisely determined that a MySpace presence would help further boost its sizable community of regular visitors and so it set about to extend the reach of its well-presented legal briefs.

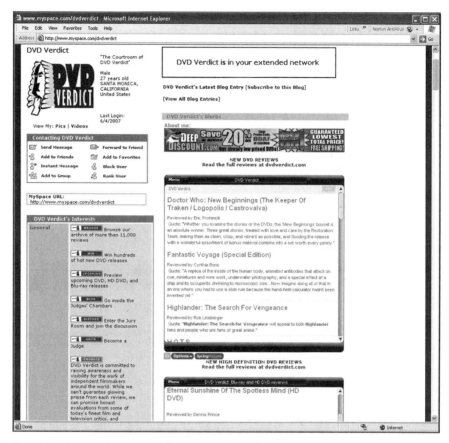

Figure 2.1 A simple but easy-to-digest space like DVD Verdict's page shows how you don't have to be a programming wizard to establish an information-rich presence that will have visitors returning day after day.

Notice the immediate presence of the company logo, that stern-looking face of its presiding magistrate, Judge Payne. The brand, then, is immediately visible and sets the tone of the site with its professional yet playfully irreverent approach to film review and product analysis (giving it that desirable edginess that attracts Net surfers). Next, notice how the content is cleanly arranged, like a prosecuting attorney's carefully laid out arguments, easy to access and completely uncluttered. With this, it's clear that DVD Verdict is all about providing compelling film and DVD reviews that can appeal to multiple demographic segments (at any age, who doesn't enjoy film, and who, in this day and age, doesn't actively indulge in DVD media?). To recap, then, here are the key success points of the DVD Verdict approach in its MySpace design:

- Conspicuous display of a memorable company brand

- Immediate expression of the company's style and approach to film and DVD analysis

- Clean and well-controlled space design that has multidemographic appeal

- Effective use of "widgets" that allow the space to be regularly updated by automated feeds of the new day's reviews

Of course, there's more going on at this particular MySpace page that is covered in Part 3, but the point here is to give quick analysis of a page approach to help you begin to consider the style and design you might employ to best effect.

MySpace Tip

Don't be afraid to *emulate* some of the page designs you see at MySpace. While you wouldn't want to outright copy an existing page, there's nothing wrong with "cherry picking" some of the better ideas that grace some of the pages you'll encounter. This is a great way to get over the blank page conundrum, allowing you to begin toying with design elements and approaches used by others that will help you springboard into what will surely become your own unique design.

So what is it that you have to offer and who do you believe will wander into your MySpace establishment to browse and buy? While you can't actively *sell* items from within a MySpace page (more on that in just a bit), you are free to actively *market* to your heart's content.

ENSURING THAT YOU'RE
NOT TONE DEAF

No, a hearing test van is not pulling up in the parking lot to test your ears for sensitivity to various "beeps" and "boops" but this is where you will determine how well you can *hear* what it is your target demographic is telling you. While you're browsing through the various pages that might be similar to what you want to launch, take heed of how popular the different pages seem to be. Although you should trust your own instincts of what design elements and layouts you like and which ones you don't (you're acting as the visitor or consumer in that regard), don't discount the buzz that seems to be present at a page that perhaps you don't entirely embrace *but others do*. How do you detect a buzz? Simply enough by taking a look at the "Friends Space" tally on the pages you visit, usually found by scrolling down a bit on a page (see Figure 2.2).

From Figure 2.2, you can see that I paid a visit to Midwest Gaming Classic's page, a destination devoted to promoting the annual electronic gaming event held in Wisconsin. The site currently has 2,182 friends. Now that's not a huge number by any means, but it's an indicator of how well MGC's page might (or might not) be working to attract folks. Also a quick look at the friends whose own MySpace page links can be seen in Figure 2.2 gives you the opportunity to learn *who* is interested in this particular page. You can visit any one of these friends' pages, then *their* friends' pages, and so on. That's how the MySpace network works.

So what about the matter of tone? Using this example, you'll find that a page's friends will likely hold similar interests, and you might visit a friend's page to see if it's commanding a larger (or maybe smaller) volume of friend traffic. Compare the various sites to see what design elements are used and how they're used to essentially "reverse engineer" why certain pages seem more attractive than

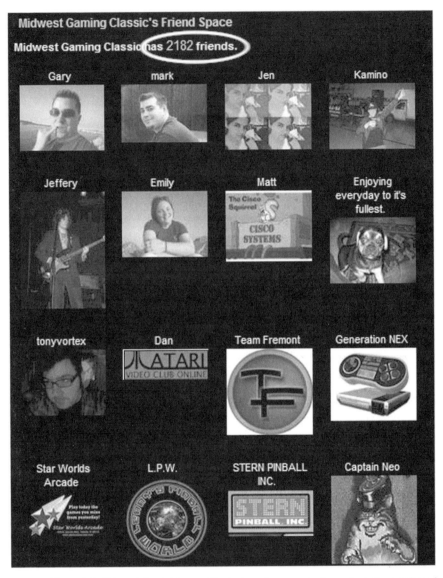

Figure 2.2 Although it might seem like just another popularity contest, the number of friends a MySpace page attracts indicates how its design might be working within the community.

others. Look for the presence of well-presented multimedia content (music content, video content, images), easy-to-navigate layout, relevancy of content, appropriateness of the language and content to the page's intent, and so on. That's where you'll discover the tone that others are using and that you, too, might want to include in your own page.

But, there's one more thing that maybe you haven't yet heard from the MySpace community: *Be yourself.* If ever there were a contradiction to the staid principles of effective target marketing, this would be it. Understand that the pervasive fabric of MySpace is that it has been built upon the tenet of self-expression. That's right—the millions of people who have established their MySpace presence have done so, at least in part, for the opportunity to just be themselves (or being the uninhibited person they *wish* they could be in the face-to-face world).

Therefore, be sure to inject plenty of yourself into your MySpace presence and avoid appearing as an opportunistic chameleon or (worse yet) a clone. This means that you'll need to spend some think-tank time listing all the surefire elements that would make your page *commercially viable* and then whittle down that list to just the key pieces and replace what you throw out with your own personality that will act as the life's blood of your effort to make the page, well, alive.

Remember that MySpace is built upon the tenets of friendship, discovery, and interaction. If you lean too heavily upon the crutch of marketing methodology, you'll risk being dismissed as purely opportunistic and, ultimately, insincere in your intentions. For example, if you're an active author who wants to harness MySpace to sell more of your books, you'll need to offer more than just a virtual card catalog of what you've written and where to buy it. While you'll definitely want to provide that information, personalize the page by explaining a bit about how you came to write each book, what you learned while authoring them, and even how you became an author. You'll likely attract other budding writers who'd be just as interested in learning how you succeeded and what information and experiences you might share that could help *them* become published someday, too. Along the way, you'll likely sell books. See how that works?

MySpace Tip

Sometimes, the fan base can do the heavy lifting for the author, developing tribute pages and groups to discuss and dissect the various elements of a writer's creations. Take, for example, the case of Stephenie Meyer, whose first work, *Twilight*, has spawned a MySpace group (groups.myspace.com/booktwilight) moderated by several enthusiasts of Meyer's modern-day supernatural tale. Although Meyer doesn't manage the group or its activities, she acknowledges the astute discussions about her characters and provides her active support of the group, even to the point of leaking excerpts from her newer works to keep the buzz active.

UNDERSTANDING THE KEY MySPACE RULES, RESTRICTIONS, AND USE LIMITATIONS

Well, you knew there'd be some sort of guidelines you'd need to adhere to as you got ready to embark on this adventure, didn't you? Although the various page construction topics covered in Part 2 of this book provide intrinsic details of the site rules, these are the main regulations you should understand and consider as you're turning your approach over and over in your head. Of course, it's unlikely that you would ever be in blatant offense of these major discouragements, but here they are just the same:

- You must be the copyright owner of copyrighted content posted on your page.

- You are prohibited from using your page to collect users' names or e-mail addresses with the intent to send unsolicited business messages.

- You are prohibited from displaying content that could be deemed offensive, racist, harassing, or exploitative.

- You are prohibited from displaying content that depicts nudity or links to adult-content Web sites.

- You are prohibited from displaying content that would reveal users' telephone numbers, e-mail addresses, or residence addresses.

- You are prohibited from displaying content that could be deemed false or libelous.

- You are prohibited from using your page for purposes of impersonating (spoofing) another user.

Offenses detected by MySpace may result in the immediate deletion of your page and account. On top of that, any verified incidents of spamming other users carry a monetary penalty of $50 per incident. This doesn't mean that you can't engage in communication with your "friends," but don't consider performing mass mailings that would be considered spam.

Beyond these rules, understand that MySpace does not allow direct sales from a page. Does this mean that you can't advertise your products, services, or other marketable works? Not at all, as you'll learn later in the best ways to create MySpace content that can engage and inform your friends and visitors of what you might offer, allowing them the ability to decide for themselves if they'd like to actively pursue your products. Fair enough?

With this, you should now have your creative juices actively flowing, swirling, and mixing to take into account all that has been discussed up to this point. In the next chapter, you'll learn about the various design elements that MySpace provides and some ways to approach the utilization of those elements to establish your design approach before actually creating your space.

Onward.

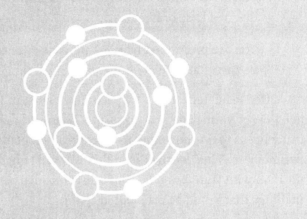

DESIGNING
FOR
MAXIMUM
RESULTS

I t's a good-news/bad-news situation that you now face: With MySpace, you're free to design your page *however you want* without many constraints from the site, yet you're also free to design your page *however you want* without any guidance in good design. The freedom to express yourself is to be wished, for sure, but it also leaves the door wide open for overt expression that many effectively torpedo your best intentions.

If you can remember the Hamster Dance or Bowling for Elves, you'll recall how budding Web designers (read: amateurs) overdid it at the outset, devising the most annoying, slow-to-load, and over-used content on the World Wide Web. Add to that the temptation indulged that resulted in garish Web design, clashing color schemes, and all manner of blinking, beeping, blitzing displays that could be clinically proven to cause seizures. We can derive from this that such control is not always best given to all comers. The same holds true in MySpace, and it's important to have some design sense and stylistic self-control if your intention is to attract a customer base.

And at MySpace there is even more to consider about the overall impression your page will make upon the audience you seek to attract and serve. That's right. Besides the way in which you decorate your MySpace establishment, you'll also need to take care in how you populate it with other MySpace friends. Although that sounds potentially exclusive or discriminatory, the fact is you need both style and clientele to establish the image that will best serve your intentions and goals. This chapter, then, discusses more specifics behind the theory of how your MySpace design should be angled, if you will, for maximum effect, not to simply impress your visitors but also to help you achieve your business goals.

KEY DESIGN CONSIDERATIONS
FOR MySPACE MARKETING

Just as any home designer will explain the dos and don'ts for achieving a certain look and feel of your residence, so too should you consider the similar guiding principles that give your MySpace page an air of good taste. First consider these recommendations as you plan your MySpace layout:

- *Not all wallpaper will wow them.* Surely you've visited many Web sites and MySpace pages that have backgrounds that assault your senses. Even if it was a cool image or color, if you had difficulty reading or otherwise deciphering the rest of the content, then it's a bad design. This applies to colors that clash or potentially absorb text (as in white text that spills onto an area of white background), textures that similarly obscure content, and even tiled images (the repeating picture) that makes it difficult for a visitor to determine what's going on besides the overbearing background.

- *Don't overload the main page.* Just as good Web design directs that your main page contain a sampling of what's in store for your visitors, so, too, should your MySpace page refrain from dumping everything on your visitors as soon as they come calling. As you'll soon learn, you can associate images, music, and video with your MySpace profile (and you should), but you should refrain from foisting *every* image, music file, and video clip on your main page. Just as a well-designed Web site uses additional pages and links to them for visitors to access additional content, the same can be done at your MySpace page. You'll learn all about this in Part 2. Just consider *underplaying* your pitch on your front page.

- *Even if you have a lot of personality, don't feel compelled to be Mr. or Mrs. PERSONALITY at MySpace.* Pardon the shouting there but, as you'll discover, some folks' pages practically scream at you when you arrive. Take a tip from one rather well-known fellow who clearly has the right to leap off your computer screen; he refrains yet still preserves who he is and what he does to his legions of fans (see Figure 3.1). The simple point is, let your work do the talking for you; don't try to overhype it with hyperactive design.

Figure 3.1 If anyone could shout about personality, it's Ashton Kutcher. Instead, notice his demure design that lets his accomplishments speak for themselves.

MySpace Tip

But, hey, if whacked out and unwieldy is what your business is all about then, by all means cut loose and do your thing. If stylish imbalance and sensory assault is what you and your target clientele are all about, go for it. Consider the guidelines just presented in case you discover you're not reaching a critical mass, though, that translates in a boost to your business. In the meantime, rock on!

- *Lighten the load on your friends.* If you overdo your MySpace page, you'll likely cause your page to clock interminably long (read: 15 seconds or more) for anyone who might have been interested enough to stop by. If you have a glut of content that takes a long time to display, visitors might often leave before it's done (and some overwrought pages have actually crashed Web browsers). You'll also learn in Part 2 about the need to maintain a quick load time for your MySpace page—thereby limiting the amount of content you'll display all at once—as well as the good effect of rotating your content to keep your page fresh.

While there's more to discuss about MySpace design tactics, these are the topmost considerations to ponder before you get too far into your page planning.

THE FIRST MySPACE MARKERS TO MANAGE

Determining the first MySpace markers to manage is probably the conundrum that faces most newcomers to the MySpace realm: where to get started and what to present upon going live. Don't fret if you have similar feelings of "performance anxiety" associated with wanting to make a good impression when you enter the MySpace fray. The fact is, it's *your space* and you're free to do with it what you like, remember? Of course, as the bent of this book is to think business and make money from a MySpace endeavor, then it's not much use to you if you're simply told, "Just relax and be yourself." You'll need to think about what you want to do ahead of time if you want to have a reasonable design ready soon after joining, So here's what to consider focusing on within your MySpace account and profile when it comes time to register and get started:

- *Name.* OK, so you might say "duh" to this one, but consider the name that you'll list on your MySpace page and whether you'll use *your* name or your business name (and I recommend the business name). And, as you'll learn in Part 2, there are options to using this field that can have a strong visual impact for your page.

- *Profile image.* Most folks insert their favorite photo booth pic, but you'll be best served to insert your business logo; be sure to have one ready.

- *Profile headline.* Consider this the "tagline" for your business's MySpace presence that will stick in your friends' and visitors' heads.

- *Background design.* A lot of money and time have been invested by marketing firms to determine how certain colors, patterns, and textures affect a browsing and buying experience. Give this one the utmost thought because this will be one of the biggest tone-setting elements of your page.

- *Profile blurb.* This is the area in your MySpace profile where you'll be entering information classified as "About Me" and so on. This is your opportunity to clearly establish the purpose and mission of your page (businesswise, that is), and it can help either welcome or discourage the folks that might pay you a visit. This is a very important element because it will communicate why you have established the space and what your visitors can expect. Consider this your five-minute elevator chat: If you had only five minutes during an elevator ride with another person, what could you tell him or her about you or your MySpace page so that this person would feel compelled to visit?

- *Blog.* Although you don't necessarily need to have this ready at the outset, there's value in establishing an initial blog entry when you open your page for visitors. Upon seeing an initial entry, your visitors will see that you intend to maintain a blog (a very good way to improve repeat visits) and they'll also be able to learn more about you, your business, and your page's intent beyond your blurb entries. If you can make this initial blog entry timely and relevant to your blurb entry, you'll communicate that you will be maintaining a fresh page that's worth visiting again and again.

MySpace Tip

Of course, the moment you register your MySpace page, *it's live*. If you registered without having a box of goods like those just mentioned, then your space will be visible in its barest existence, unadorned and unrefined, for the MySpace community (and even unregistered visitors) to see. This is beyond simplicity; it's downright premature in design, and it might be advisable to keep the windows papered at this nascent stage. To that end, consider making your page *private* for a time. Just as a new business readying for grand opening in the nearest strip mall, it makes good business sense to keep your doors locked until you're ready for the dramatic announcement that you have arrived (see Figure 3.2). Look to Chapter 4 where you'll learn about how setting your space to "private" is achieved but, for the point of this discussion, consider taking this approach until you're absolutely ready to make your big splash.

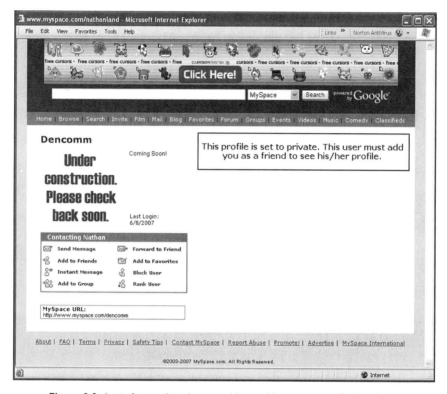

Figure 3.2 Just after registering, consider making your page "private" as a way to indicate that you're not yet quite ready to entertain visitors.

LOOKING ISN'T ENOUGH

Finally, to wrap up this planning discussion and ready you to begin your actual MySpace registration and page construction, pay heed to these thoughts about your expectations of a MySpace page and what you may need to do to achieve your purpose. The buzz about MySpace, of course, is the notion of popularity—having an impressively high number of friends who regularly hang out at your page.

But popularity, in business terms, is only as good as the *conversion rate* that it brings. That is, if you take this notion into the realm of a brick-and-mortar business, it's great that your store is full of browsers, but it doesn't do you a lick of good if nobody buys anything. You'd be bearing all the costs to run a business—in the MySpace realm this largely consists of time but, then, we know that time is money—without any income to offset those costs, let alone gain a profit. What this means is that you'll need to consider a few more things to ensure that your MySpace endeavor delivers a return on your investment. So ponder the following:

- *What is the purpose of your MySpace page?* If this sounds like a silly question, it's really not. Before you even begin planning your MySpace design, you need to have a solid reason for *why* you will create a page and *what* you expect it to do for you and your business. Think hard about this because establishing and maintaining a useful MySpace page does entail commitment, creatively and time-wise, and you want to be sure that the energy you expend isn't for nothing.

- *How much time will you and can you spend maintaining your MySpace page?* This touches on the previous item regarding the purpose of your page and, in support of that, how much time investment will be required to satisfy that purpose? Will you have that much time, assuming it will be significant? This matter, then, might very well drive the purpose and content of your page, scaled back out of necessity to account for the level of maintenance you're prepared to give it (and understand that many of the business and big company or personality pages are maintained by a dedicated individual or team).

- *How fresh can you keep your MySpace page?* Another spoke on the "purpose" and "maintenance" wheels here is where you determine how often and by how much you'll be modifying the content of your MySpace page. Knowing that regularly updated content is what draws the most active traffic, you'll need to be sure that you'll have enough time to add or make changes on a regular basis. Of course, if you determine that you can be successful with infrequent updates (perhaps just once a week?), this could solve any conflicts with the amount of time you can spend on your page.

- *How will you extend the use of your MySpace page?* This goes back to the "purpose" topic yet takes your train of thought in a slightly different direction as you consider how your MySpace page will figure into your *overall* business plan and collection of business resources that will work together to help you attain your goals. Remembering that you are not allowed to sell goods *directly* from a MySpace page (for the time being, anyway; there's chatter that this might change in the near future), you need to establish an appropriate "role" that your page will fulfill to drive customers to the point of purchase (think of the roadside sign twirlers that direct drivers to a place of business; same thing). But while your page is performing the "visibility" purpose for your business, what else can it offer to visitors? Bands offer free downloads of their current songs; filmmakers offer free clips from their latest features; businesses offer bulletins about upcoming product releases and special offers and also provide exclusive coupons to their MySpace visitors. Get it?

Understandably, this chapter poses many, many questions for you to ponder, but they're important to consider and respond to. Although you might be eager to dive into your account creation, pause for a while to think about all that has been covered in the first three chapters of this book. The better prepared you are with your approach plan, the better your initial results will be when you begin constructing your page.

ESTABLISHING YOUR **MySPACE** PRESENCE

SIGNING UP WITH MySPACE

And now, without further ado, it's time to begin creating your own MySpace page. You'll soon see that the MySpace registration and profile tools are rather intuitive and that creating a page is relatively straightforward—relatively. You'll also discover that there is much you can do to truly personalize your page and develop it specifically for meeting your business goals. Therefore, as you go along through this part of the book, you'll learn about the customizations you can make that will quickly and easily guide you beyond many of the "normal folks" who use the site largely to chat and play.

With that said, let's begin by your getting registered.

As of this writing there are up to 183,747,455 registered MySpace accounts. In this exercise, you'll see how your account will add to that tally, one that grows by the minute to the tune of about 230,000 new accounts each day. Don't feel as if you're late to the party, though, or as if you'll be positioned far to the back of the line; you'll learn how to slingshot yourself in front of many others so your space will get noticed properly. For now, open your favorite Web browser and navigate to www.myspace.com.

MySpace Tip

Lest we assume anything here, you'll need to bring a few things to MySpace in order create an account. First, you'll need a computer with an active connection to the Internet. Next, you'll need a Web browser application to use for navigating the Web (and for MySpace use, it's recommended that PC users utilize MS Internet Explorer or Mozilla Firefox; Macintosh users are best served by Firefox or Safari), and you'll also need an active e-mail account. These are all very basic elements of utilizing the Internet, and likely you've got these bases well covered as you read this.

Upon arriving at the MySpace home page, you'll see the conspicuously placed invitation to *Login* or *Sign Up!* If you're a new user, click on the *Sign Up!* button (see Figure 4.1).

The next screen you'll see asks for some key information, but not *all* of it is required for you to effectively create a MySpace account (see Figure 4.2).

Within the *Join MySpace Here!* fill-in form, here's what you'll need to provide:

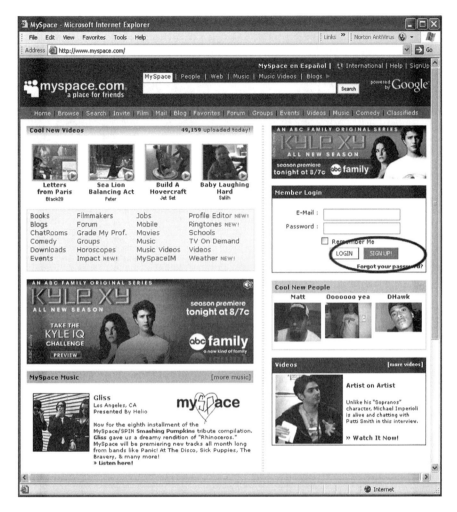

Figure 4-1. It begins easily enough from the MySpace home page. Sign up by clicking on the appropriately labeled button.

- *E-mail address.* Provide a valid e-mail address so that MySpace will be able to contact you and confirm that the address isn't some bogus or illicit account being created. Additionally, you'll need to respond to an initial e-mail message from MySpace before you can begin the "friending" process or post comments and bulletins.

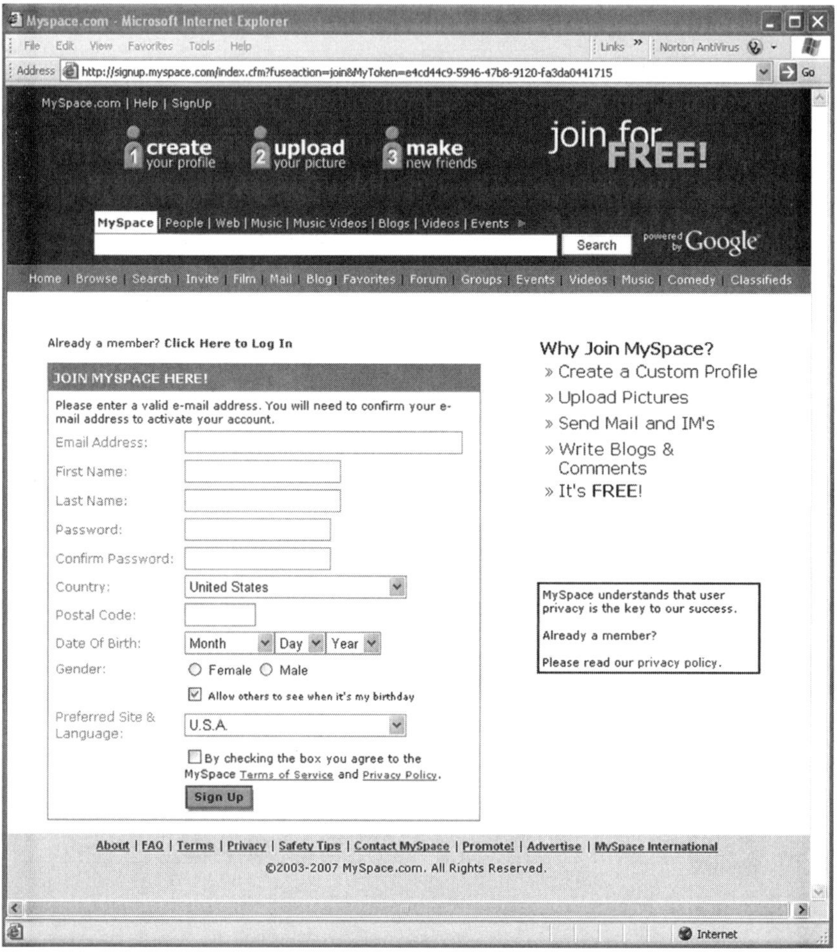

Figure 4-2. On the first sign-up page, enter a valid e-mail address and an account password. The other information, you'll learn, is up to you to make accurate or "close enough."

- *First name.* This will be the display name that shows at the top of your MySpace page (and if you refer back to Figure 3.2, you'll see that I used my intended business name, Dencomm). You can enter your actual first name if you like; you can change this entry at any time in the future.

- *Last name.* Entering something in this field isn't required, and many MySpace users prefer not to enter their actual surnames for privacy purposes. Something entered in this field will be searchable by the MySpace community, so if you *want* to have your last name searchable, then enter it. Otherwise, consider entering your business name a second time or another relevant term that could pop up in user searches.

- *Password.* Create a password that will ensure that only *you* can access the maintenance elements of your account. The best passwords are those that include a combination of letters and numbers. In fact, MySpace requires that you establish a password that includes at least one number. Other password safeguards include using a combination of capitalized and lower-case letters plus numbers. What-ever you choose, enter it in this field.

- *Confirm password.* For your own benefit, MySpace requests that you enter your chosen password a second time, just to confirm it.

- *Country.* MySpace cannot actually verify this, but since you're looking to establish a viable presence in a market, choose the appropriate country name from the drop-down menu.

- *Postal code.* Again, this is not something that MySpace veri-fies, but you are required to enter a five-digit number here. If you're hoping to attract MySpace users to a local business establishment you own and operate, it's to your advantage to use the real postal code for those who might search their area for you and your services (such as eateries, coffee shops, small venues, and so on).

- *Date of birth.* It's expected that the majority of MySpace users lie about their age here, and that's mostly OK—*mostly*. You're free to choose any month-day-year combination, but understand that if your age calculates to be less than 18, MySpace will automatically make your page private and thus accessible only by those you have friended (not a good idea for a business). More importantly, if your selections indicate you're under the age of 14, you're in violation of

MySpace's terms regarding under-aged users, and your account will be subject to deletion. And, if you're over 18 yet "pose" as under in order to make contact with younger users, you're in violation of MySpace's policy to thwart online predators (a criminal offense, by the way). That said, it's OK to choose an age that keeps you within your target demographic, but, if you can muster it (and I think you can), use your real age.

- *Gender.* There are just two choices, so pick the one that best describes you as proprietor of your business page.

- *"Allow others to see when it's my birthday" check box.* Although many users fudge their actual birth year, many will specify the accurate month and day. Many MySpace users enjoy sending birthday wishes, and, if that sounds fun to you, check this box (and know that some business operators put in the "birth" of their business here, proudly celebrating how many years they've been in business).

- *Preferred site and language,* No need to be cagey here; just select the proper MySpace site and language setting.

- *"Terms" and "policy" check box.* Read the *Terms of Use* and *Privacy Policy* carefully. Then click on this check box to indicate that you understand and will abide by the rules in order to proceed with the creation of your account.

OK. Talking about those fields probably took longer than it will to actually fill them in, but now you're clear about their use and potential abuse. Fill in the fields appropriately, and click on the *Sign Up* button at the bottom of the page. When you do, you'll be directed to a security screen that prompts you to type in the scrambled letters you see displayed (see Figure 4.3); this prevents Web "bots" from programmatically creating accounts for whatever purpose and ensures that only actual people can sign up. Enter the letters or numbers you see, and click on the *Continue to My Account* button.

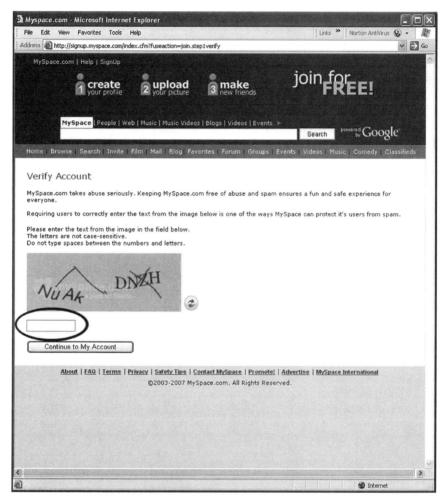

Figure 4-3. Type in the graphically represented letters (or numbers) you see on the security screen so that you can continue creating your MySpace account.

At this point, MySpace is ready to help you upload a photo for your new account and, if you have that ready now, click the *Browse* button to search your computer and select the image of your choice (see Figure 4.4). Once you've selected the image file on your computer, click on the *Upload* button to add it to your account. If you're not yet ready with an image, that's fine too and you only need to click on the *Skip for now* text link you see in Figure 4.4.

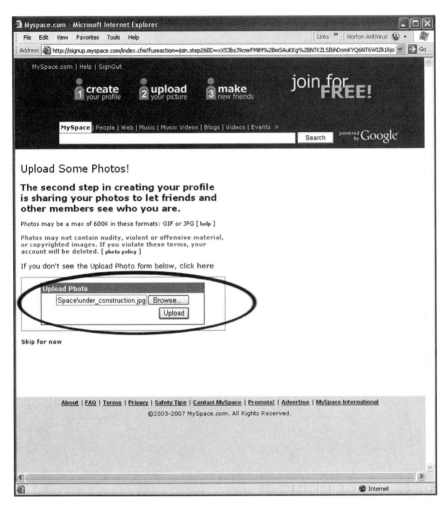

Figure 4-4. If you have a profile image to upload, enter it in this screen. If you don't, don't worry since you can upload one later.

MySpace Tip

Although it has been recommended you have all of your initial elements ready—images, music files, video, and so on—when you register with MySpace, we'll take the approach here that those elements aren't yet available. In this way, you can see how to start from a bare minimum when you register and then discover how to return to your profile to make customizations. If you prefer to be fully prepared at the outset, go ahead and read through the chapters in this part of the book so that you can develop your own checklist of information and whatnot that you'll want and need for a fully dressed go-live of your page. I've split the difference somewhat by having prepared an "under construction" image to upload.

Next, although you're not being pressured, MySpace is ready to help you get the word out to your friends that your new page is launching. If you have e-mail addresses of friends and you want to let them in on the ground floor, so to speak, you can enter those addresses plus a message to invite folks you know to your page right away. Again, if this notice is premature for your plan, click on the *Skip for now* text at the bottom of the screen you see in Figure 4.5.

And now—*ta da!*—you have a MySpace page, sort of. As you can see in Figure 4.6, MySpace has accepted the information I submitted to create the barest representation of the Dencomm page. Immediately, notice the two action boxes (circled in Figure 4.6). The topmost box asks you to visit your specified e-mail account to locate and respond to the message sent from MySpace; this is the step necessary to begin friending, posting comments to other friends, and creating page bulletins. For the sake of this step in the account creation process, this will be delayed until the discussion in Chapter 7. On the other hand, the other highlighted action box in Figure 4.6 requires immediate attention.

Notice that MySpace is prompting you to establish a *Name/URL*. This is where you can create your own universal resource locator (URL) for your page (the Web address folks will use to visit your page directly). Click on the text, *Click Here*, to begin the URL naming process.

As you can see in Figure 4.7, you'll be taken to another form page where you can craft your own URL for your page. It's advisable to do this right away lest someone else claim the URL you had

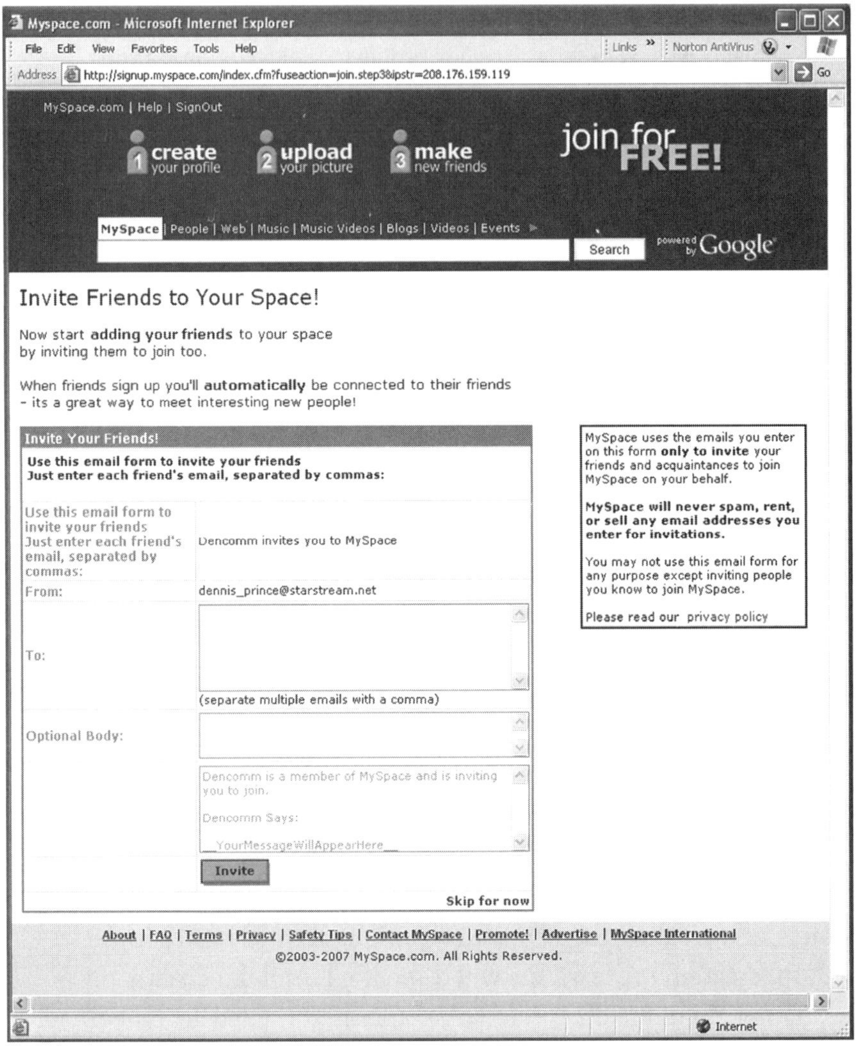

Figure 4.5 If you're ready to let some folks you know in on the fact that you have a new MySpace page, you can craft that announcement here. If not, skip it for now.

hoped to establish for yourself. Of course, unless your business or endeavor name is something potentially common such as "Daisy's Place" or "Movie Madness" or something like that, you'll likely not encounter too much trouble getting the URL you want. For this example, I've chosen to establish a URL that is identical to my

Figure 4.6 You're practically through the first phase of your MySpace setup. Just establish your unique MySpace URL and, later, you'll confirm your e-mail address so that you can begin "friending."

page's name, Dencomm. Therefore, where prompted, I entered "dencomm" to the MySpace URL, establishing my page with a URL of www.myspace.com/dencomm. Click on the *Submit* button to confirm your URL selection.

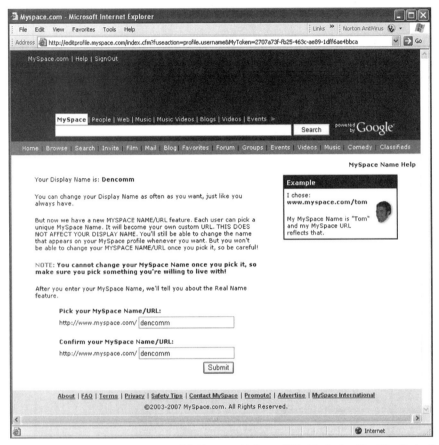

Figure 4.7 Don't delay in establishing your MySpace URL; it's the key identifier that will help folks find your business-extended presence within the community.

MySpace Tip

So what happens if the URL you want is already taken? Well, it's easy to secure something similar to www.myspace.com /moviemadness for yourself by adding numbers or under-scores to your URL (such as "moviemadness07" or "movie_madness") but that's not a very good idea. If you take this route, your URL *will* be unique, but it will be semantically and syntactically similar to another page and potentially confusing to the MySpace community. Instead, I recommend that you take a different direction to ensure true uniqueness and ensure that your MySpace URL will be memorable (such as "MovieDen" or "InsaneCinema" or something like that).

When MySpace confirms the uniqueness of your URL, you'll receive a pop-up box (see Figure 4.8) that asks you to be absolutely certain that this is the URL you want because there's no changing it after this point. You will not be able to change this URL, and your only way to abandon it will be to close your MySpace account and create an all new one. Click on the *OK* button to confirm your chosen URL. When you do this, you'll get *another* pop-up box reiterating that you cannot change this URL once it's assigned. It's all right—click on *OK*.

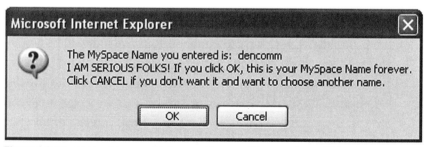

Figure 4.8 Be prepared to *completely* commit yourself to your chosen URL. Once you set it, MySpace asserts, it's set for the life of your account. Be certain.

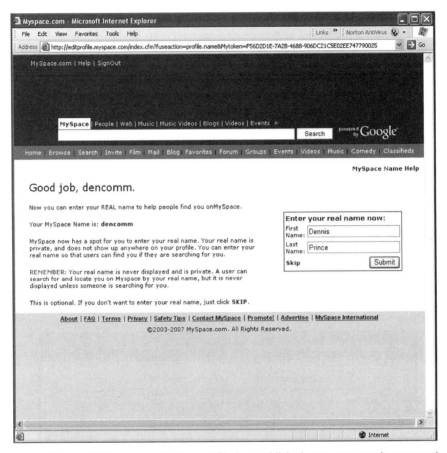

Figure 4.9 Once your MySpace URL is established, you can supply your real name to assist MySpace users in finding you by your given name as well as by your business persona.

It may seem to be pushy about the matter, but MySpace again offers you the opportunity to establish your *real* name to be associated with your account (see Figure 4.9). Recall that the first and last name you entered back in Figure 4.2 was associated with the *display name* of your MySpace page, and it was expected that you didn't enter your real name at that time. Now, you *can* enter your given name and rest assured that MySpace will maintain utmost privacy of it in association with your account. Then again, if you do enter your actual name, it will be searchable by users as a way for them to locate a page you have created (such as if your proud mother searched on your name to see if you have a MySpace page; and if so and it's a page that wouldn't make your mother proud, then skip this step by clicking on the *Skip* text).

Of course, I'm very proud to be establishing my Dencomm page, and I know that my mother would smile wide when she finds it. Therefore, I chose to enter my real name and clicked on the *Submit* button. When I did, MySpace displayed a confirmation page like the one shown in Figure 4.10. And, if ever I changed my mind about having my real name associated with my account, I could change it whenever I desired. Oh, and notice that if you're a user of America Online's Instant Messenger (AIM) service, MySpace

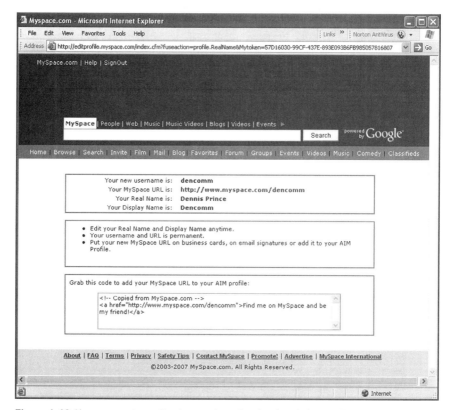

Figure 4-10 Your account creation is complete, for the time being, and you can now extend news of your MySpace presence to AOL Instant Messenger users.

provides a bit of easy code to add to your AIM signature line that will reveal your new MySpace page URL.

As a final point of confirmation, notice how MySpace provides an active link to my page URL as shown in Figure 4.10; I can see that www.myspace.com/dencomm is an active link, and when I click on it, I'll be routed to my actual page as it stands now, visible in Figure 4.11.

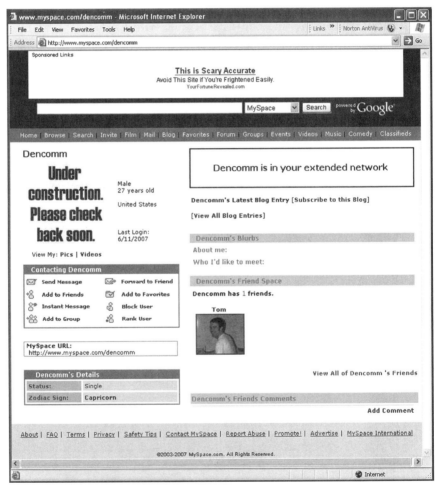

Figure 4.11 It's a done deal, and now you're looking at the starter page you've created. You'll want to get to work to spruce it up pretty quickly.

And there it is; the job one is done. Pat yourself on the back for having leaped into the buzzing realm of MySpace. Next up, in Chapter 5, you'll learn about the hot topic at MySpace—privacy and security. Although you're probably eager to dress up your page, first things first: Let's keep your efforts safe and sane *before* you invest too much time in it. Once that's done, you'll move along to discover how you can make adjustments and customizations to your space to make it better reflect you and your goals.

MySpace Tip

With this completed, you might be tempted to speak up and say this is all quite straightforward and hardly in need of a written explanation. Maybe so, but since I'm working from the understanding that you're new to MySpace and that, perhaps, you haven't visited the site before reading this, it makes sense to explain the foundational aspects of the site. From here, the discussion can proceed with the expectation that you're familiar with the core terminology of the site, making the subsequent discussions about customizing your page much easier. The journey to making money begins with a first step, and, congratulations, you've just succeeded in taking it.

SECURING
YOUR
SPACE

I n the previous chapter, you created your MySpace page and readied yourself to begin setting up shop. But just as you would secure the front door to a strip mall pad where you hope to entertain visitors-to-be, so too should you ensure that the door to your page is secured until such time as you're ready to welcome guests. In the realm of MySpace, this means that you'll want to keep your space locked down and even away from curious eyes *until you're ready*. This is easy enough to do, but, if not done, you might find difficulty in shooing away looky-loos while you're trying to get established. And, beyond this, you'll also want to ensure that *you're* safe as you work odd hours, perhaps, to get your space spruced up. In this chapter, you'll learn about security, privacy, and "controlled release" at MySpace.

DRAWING THE CURTAINS UNTIL YOU'RE DRESSED

If you want to keep out the Peeping Toms until you're really ready to be seen, here are some of the first things you should do with your MySpace account to give you a bit of breathing room so that you will be able to adorn your page before unveiling it to curious passersby. Since you now have a MySpace account of your own, visit www.myspace.com, enter your e-mail address and password, and then click on the *Login* button (see Figure 5.1).

Once you've logged in, you'll be redirected to your MySpace profile page where you can see your current page layout plus have visible access to various editing tools and links (see Figure 5.2).

MySpace Tip

Once you're logged into your account, you can navigate away from your MySpace page, and, if you return to the MySpace home page, it will recognize you and keep your account log in active. This is good news and bad news. The good news is that you won't have to enter your e-mail and password if you temporarily navigate away from the site and then back again. Beware, though, that if you use a shared computer or access your MySpace account from a public access computer (such as at a university or public library), unless you log out of your account, it will remain available for editing by *anyone* who

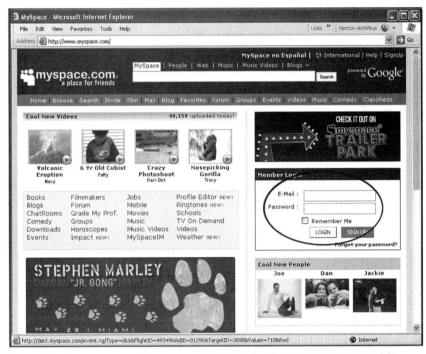

Figure 5.1 After your account has been established, log in on each subsequent visit when you wish to make changes to your profile and settings.

Figure 5.2 When you access your account, you'll see this collection of MySpace editing tools.

MySpace en Español | International | MySpace.com | Help | SignOut

Figure 5.3 For safety's sake, be sure to sign out of your MySpace account before you step away from a shared or public computer.

might take up the keyboard and mouse after you've stepped away. Best bet: Use a secure computer or be sure to click the *SignOut* text link found at the top of the MySpace account page (see Figure 5.3).

So, in order to prevent anyone from watching you create your space or generally to keep folks from peeking as your page changes bit by bit while it's still a work in progress, set your account to *Private*. To achieve this, click on the text link, *Account Settings*, which you can see in Figure 5.2. When you do, you'll navigate to the Change Account Settings screen where you will then click on the *Change Settings* text link to the right of the Privacy Settings row (see Figure 5.4).

Next, you'll be directed to the Privacy Settings screen where you can set the Who Can View My Profile control to *My Friends Only* by simply clicking on the appropriate button (see Figure 5.5). Click on the *Change Settings* button at the bottom of the screen, and you're done. With this complete, your page display will have the same look as you saw in Figure 3.2, the banner clearly stating that your profile is set to private and only those folks you accepted as friends will be able to see your "live" page (and you'll delay accepting and entertaining friends until your setup is complete).

One last item to consider at the beginning of your MySpace adventure is whether the e-mail address you used when you signed up is the e-mail address you want to associate with your page going forward. Perhaps you created your page with a personal e-mail account and later decided that it would be a good idea to create a business-specific e-mail account to accompany your page (a good

Figure 5.4 Your first visit to the Change Account Settings screen should be to make your page private in order to give you time to set up before you open your page to the public.

idea, indeed). It's fine with MySpace if you make this change, but you will have to go through one more e-mail confirmation step just to ensure that the new address you give is valid.

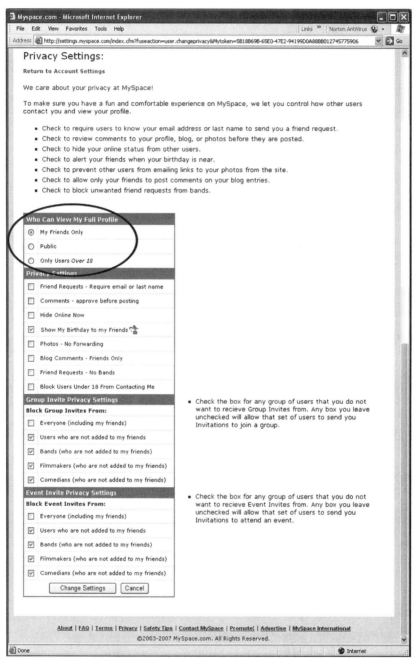

Figure 5.5 Change your privacy setting with a simple selection of a button so you can work on your page away from curious eyes.

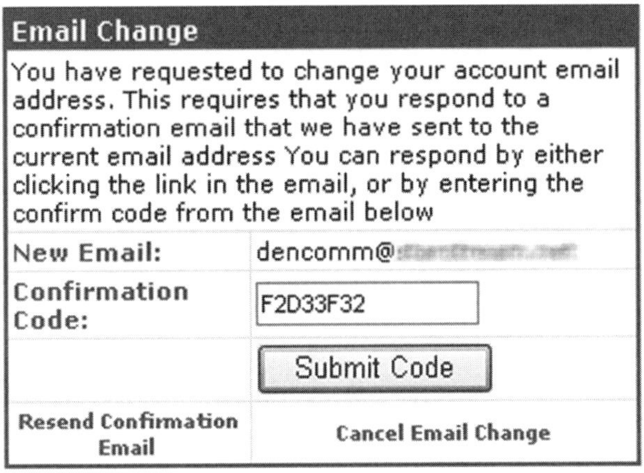

Email Change

You have requested to change your account email address. This requires that you respond to a confirmation email that we have sent to the current email address You can respond by either clicking the link in the email, or by entering the confirm code from the email below

New Email:	dencomm@
Confirmation Code:	F2D33F32
	Submit Code
Resend Confirmation Email	Cancel Email Change

Figure 5.6 You can change your account's e-mail address at any time, but you'll need to confirm the change with the code that MySpace will send to you.

To do this, simply remove the existing e-mail address visible in the Change Account Settings screen (refer again to Figure 5.4) and enter the new e-mail address you wish to use. Once that is done, click on the *Change* button at the bottom of the screen. Immediately, you'll see an Email Change confirmation box (see Figure 5.6) where you'll be prompted to enter a confirmation code that was sent to the new e-mail address you specified. Enter that confirmation code in the appropriate box and click on the *Submit Code* button (or you can cancel the e-mail change by clicking on the text, *Cancel Email Change*).

UNDERSTANDING THE REST OF THE PRIVACY SETTINGS

There are several more privacy settings available to you. Here's a look at each and how they might be best utilized for you and your business as you expand into the realm of MySpace (refer to Figure 5.7).

Privacy Settings	
☐	Friend Requests - Require email or last name
☐	Comments - approve before posting
☐	Hide Online Now
☑	Show My Birthday to my Friends 🐾
☐	Photos - No Forwarding
☐	Blog Comments - Friends Only
☐	Friend Requests - No Bands
☐	Block Users Under 18 From Contacting Me

Group Invite Privacy Settings

Block Group Invites From:

☐	Everyone (including my friends)
☑	Users who are not added to my friends
☑	Bands (who are not added to my friends)
☑	Filmmakers (who are not added to my friends)
☑	Comedians (who are not added to my friends)

Event Invite Privacy Settings

Block Event Invites From:

☐	Everyone (including my friends)
☑	Users who are not added to my friends
☑	Bands (who are not added to my friends)
☑	Filmmakers (who are not added to my friends)
☑	Comedians (who are not added to my friends)

[Change Settings] [Cancel]

Figure 5.7 Take a look, now, at the rest of the privacy settings available in MySpace.

"Privacy Settings"

- *Friend requests.* These require e-mail or last name: Many, many folks will want to become "friends" with you and your page but, truth be told, some are just trying to beef up their own friend counts (for posterity's sake or whatever). While it's best for a business concern to not discriminate, you can check this box if you want a little more assuredness that your friends are truly "friends"—they'll be prompted by MySpace to provide your last name or e-mail address to confirm that they really know you. Best advice going in is to leave this unchecked, and, if it becomes a problem later, you can always enable it.

- *Comments—approve before posting.* Once you've "friended" someone, that person is able to post comments about your page in a way that is visible in the Comments section of your page. While this person does have to be accepted by you to be included in your friends list, his or her comments are not initially subject to similar screening before they are posted to your page for all other visitors to see. It's a good idea to check this box just as you'd likely screen anything posted on a public bulletin board within your brick-and-mortar business. If you read something that is objectionable to you or that you think would be to the rest of your clientele, this gives you the ability to delete it.

- *Hide online now.* By default, a little "online now" icon is displayed on your MySpace page whenever you're logged into your page for housekeeping and other editing. It's a good way to let folks know that you're "at home," and it could prompt them to step up and make contact. If you prefer to keep the shades drawn while you're in your shop, check the box, and the "online now" icon will not be displayed.

- *Show my birthday to my friends.* During the sign-up exercise you learned about this feature—your friends will be alerted when your birthday arrives (based upon the date-of-birth information you provided during sign up). Keep this checked if you want to celebrate with others or uncheck it if you prefer to keep this on the mum. Remember, it's often a good idea to announce and celebrate your business's birthday publicly, potentially tying the event with a special offer, sale, or other such enticement.

- *Photos—no forwarding.* By default, the pictures you post within the *View My: Pics* area of your page can be easily e-mailed to others; visitors seeing them may decide that a friend of theirs might be interested in seeing the photo, too. For a business concern, it is a good idea to keep this box unchecked since it would allow your visitors to forward an image (of a product or something?) to another person they think might be interested. This is part of the word-of-mouth dynamic and enabling the photo forwarding could entice another person to come visit your space.

- *Blog comments—friends only.* The only thing you can be certain about in the online realm is how uncertain you are about what others might write. If you're hosting a blog at your space and you open it up for others to comment in a public fashion, who knows what they might write? Unless you open blogs intended for interactivity (a good idea, usually), check this box for any blogging where the conversation is one way: from you to your visitors.

- *Friend requests—no bands.* While this might initially sound confusing to block, requests from users identified as being affiliated with a band can lead to a massive flood of band-centric requests from budding musicians eager to stuff virtual handbills into the mitts of anyone passing by. If you want to avoid this, check this box. If you're up for looking for tunesmiths who might be pushing their next gig, leave it unchecked. Only you can determine if this is suitable to your page.

- *Block users under 18 from contacting me.* Maybe you want to screen out the kiddies (if your business doesn't cater to them) or you have content of a nature that is not appropriate for youngsters (such as if you're operating a tavern where only those 21 and older are allowed). If this is the case, then go ahead and check this box. Otherwise, keep it unchecked to determine how much draw your page has for the younger set (a study in demographics that could be quite valuable to you in the long run).

"Group Invite Privacy Settings—Block Group Invites From:"

"Groups" at MySpace are subcommunities of members who share a common interest and enjoy hobnobbing with one another in pursuit of their passion. To build their group size, group owners will invite MySpace members whose profiles reveal that they might be of a like mind. You can open your page and be subject to invitations although you may need to fend off irrelevant entreaties. As you can see from the blocking options (below and in Figure 5.7), you can screen some or all group invitations as you desire:

- Everyone (including my friends)
- Users who are not added to my friends
- Bands (who are not added to my friends)
- Filmmakers (who are not added to my friends)
- Comedians (who are not added to my friends)

Later, though, you might determine that hosting a group of your own could be good for improving the reach of your business (more on that in Chapter 10).

"Event Invite Privacy Settings—Block Event Invites From:"

Much like the group function, events can be announced within the MySpace community and be broadcast throughout the population as metered by these privacy settings. Just as with groups, determine how you want to be notified of events as you enter the MySpace fray:

- Everyone (including my friends)

- Users who are not added to my friends

- Bands (who are not added to my friends)

- Filmmakers (who are not added to my friends)

- Comedians (who are not added to my friends)

Oh, and look to Chapter 10 for a discussion of heralding your own events.

ADDITIONAL ACCOUNT SETTINGS TO MAKE YOUR PAGE SECURE

Before we leave this discussion on security and privacy settings, here are a few more account-level settings you can toggle on and off as it suits the needs of you and your business (refer to Figure 5.8).

- *E-mail address.* Although this has already been discussed from the perspective of changing your e-mail address to one most suitable to your business, recognize that you can change your e-mail address any time you feel it's necessary. Besides better business alignment and e-mail segregation (business from personal), consider changing your referenced e-mail address if you think it has somehow "become written on the bathroom wall" and you're receiving a high

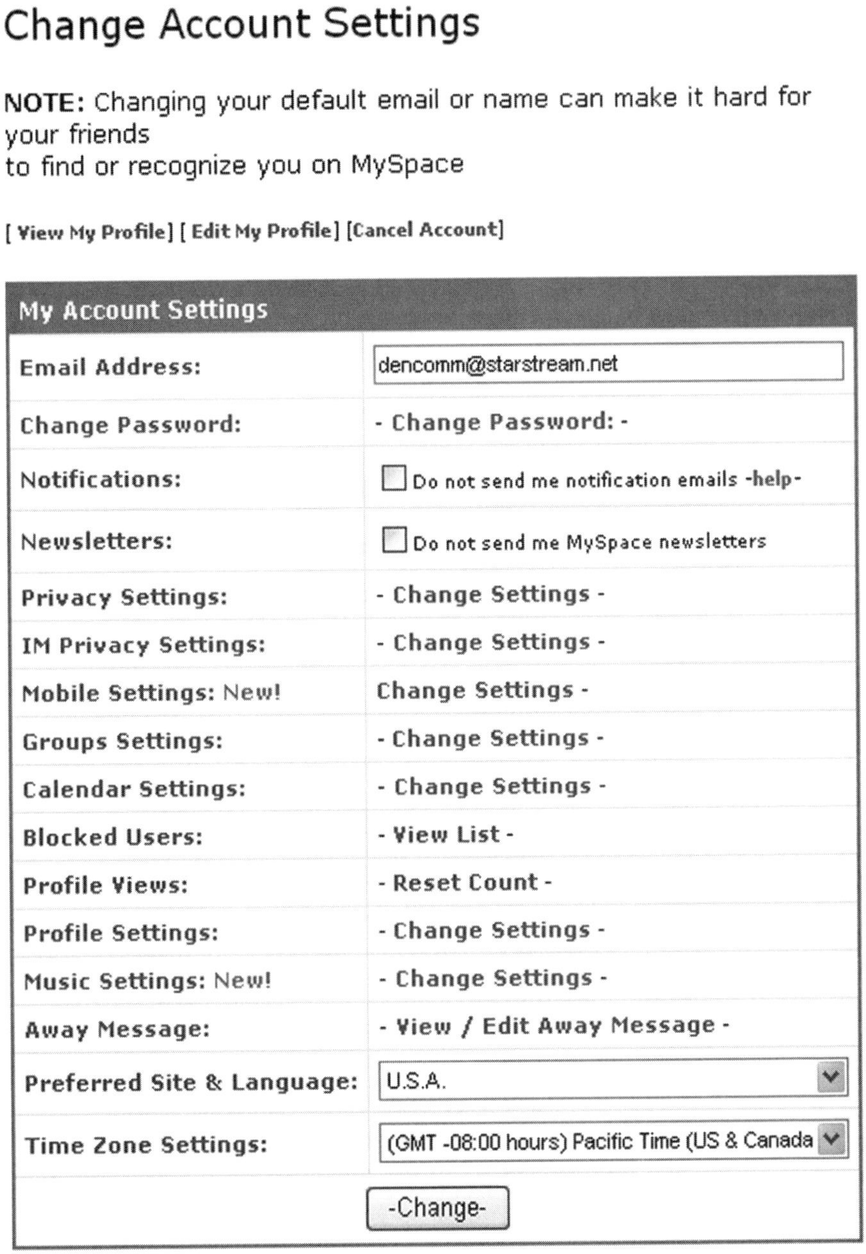

Change Account Settings

NOTE: Changing your default email or name can make it hard for your friends
to find or recognize you on MySpace

[View My Profile] [Edit My Profile] [Cancel Account]

My Account Settings	
Email Address:	dencomm@starstream.net
Change Password:	- Change Password: -
Notifications:	☐ Do not send me notification emails -help-
Newsletters:	☐ Do not send me MySpace newsletters
Privacy Settings:	- Change Settings -
IM Privacy Settings:	- Change Settings -
Mobile Settings: New!	Change Settings -
Groups Settings:	- Change Settings -
Calendar Settings:	- Change Settings -
Blocked Users:	- View List -
Profile Views:	- Reset Count -
Profile Settings:	- Change Settings -
Music Settings: New!	- Change Settings -
Away Message:	- View / Edit Away Message -
Preferred Site & Language:	U.S.A.
Time Zone Settings:	(GMT -08:00 hours) Pacific Time (US & Canada
	-Change-

Figure 5.8 At the profile level, note the additional settings that serve to better control
the privacy and suitability aspects of your MySpace page.

volume of spam or other bothersome messages. Under-stand, though, the impact of changing your e-mail address can have on bona fide contacts and customers; they would need to be notified of the switch.

- *Change password.* Be sure you change your MySpace account password at the first moment you suspect your account has been compromised (e.g., perhaps someone has learned your password and is actively making changes to your account). A good way to stay ahead of the potential for this is to establish a regular interval when you intentionally change your password, at least every six months is the usual recommendation.

- *IM privacy settings.* Instant messaging (IM) is one of the attractions of MySpace for many in its community; it pro-vides the ability to exchange chat-type messages in real time whenever members are online (recall the Online Now indicator). The settings you can modify here include a filter where no one can IM you, only your friends can IM you, or anyone can IM you. In addition, much like the groups and bulletins settings, you can also filter out the sorts of invites you receive to become "IM-able" to other community members that might seek you out. You'll need to decide how strict you want to maintain your level of "interruptability" while on MySpace and give careful con-sideration to the potential value of being live to entertain your target audience and their inquiries.

- *Mobile settings.* If being connected and responsive while on the go is important to your business goals, consider estab-lishing a linkage within MySpace to have messages routed directly to your mobile device. You'll read about the details of this process in Chapter 6, but, for now, consider how this might work to boost your presence and interactivity to the benefit of your business.

A FINAL WORD ON YOUR MySPACE SECURITY SETTINGS

Remember that any of the privacy and account settings you establish can be changed. When you're ready to open your page for public consumption, you make your page *un*-private again. Any other settings you enable can as easily be changed as your needs and your business direction dictate. The flexibility to manage your settings at MySpace is one of the key reasons it is such a valuable tool within your business presence portfolio. That said, your previously established account is now secured. Turn the page to Chapter 6 to learn how to begin crafting a personality for your page.

CUSTOMIZING YOUR MySPACE PRESENCE

Finally, it's time to add flair and style to your MySpace page. The front door is duly locked, allowing you to toil away without being distracted by comments or suggestions by others. Here you can experiment with all sorts of design elements to make your page ready for visitors. The basic MySpace page look is rather antiseptic and perhaps too conservative for your taste, so here you can work with layouts, fonts, colors, content, and more to develop a page that you think will best represent you and your business. Note that there are many ways to dress up your site—in content as well in approach—so this chapter introduces some of the most common methods available for customizing your page. The goal here is to get your hands a bit dirty with all the fun, establish a nongeneric look to your page, and open the door for you to further experiment on your own. Let's get started.

A QUICK LOOK AT THE TOOL SET

It's time to see what's available in the tool shed for changing around the look and feel of your MySpace. The good news is that there are many different tools you can use to achieve some interesting looks, from basic-yet-beneficial to completely "da bomb." As each tool set is discussed, think about what each can deliver and which would deliver the look and style that will best attract and hook your target audience. If simple design will be most satisfactory to your clientele, then you might have a pretty easy go of it. If you feel the need to get fancier to properly position yourself in a visible situation in the community, then you might need to roll up your sleeves and spend a bit more time at it. Again, consider your audience in all this while also accounting for the level of maintenance required—in terms of tool use and design result—as you approach customizing.

Basic MySpace Tools

When you login to your MySpace account (refer back to Figure 5.1), you'll access your profile management page where you'll find simple forms that will help you perform simple modifications (see Figure 6.1). Mostly, these are text entry blocks where you can add information about you and your business; they are not so much about modifying the actual *look* of the elements as they appear on the page. Even so, you'll find out how you can utilize other methods within the simple MySpace forms where you will be able to create some rather spiffy effects.

Slinging HTML and CSS Code

If there are certain pages you've been admiring in the MySpace community, expect that the majority of the people who created these pages have employed the use of actual *coding*. The mere mention of the word "coding" is often enough to send casual Netgoers running away screaming, fearful that they'll be exposed as

Figure 6.1 From your MySpace account page, you'll be able to begin editing your profile in order to customize your community presence.

woefully inadequate in this new age of computer-programmed lifestyles. Relax. Although many of the great effects you see are code-driven, the fact is that they utilize simple code statements that are easily used by novices just like you. As we go along, you'll learn about HTML (hypertext markup language) and CSS (cascading style sheets) "statements" that you can plug into your MySpace profile to achieve a look that's impressive.

While this book can't ever aspire to train you deeply in these coding styles, you'll learn enough to improve you page's look. Look to the appendix for a couple of good books about HTML and CSS if you get the urge to learn more.

Turning to Third-Party Profile Generators

As popular and prevalent as MySpace has become, it's natural that it would spawn a niche market of profile customizing "helpers." There is a variety of online Web sites dedicated to providing you with easy ways to develop a customized look for your page (actually providing you the code that you'll insert into the appropriate MySpace profile fields). Later in this chapter you'll learn how to locate a profile generator for yourself, and you'll see a demonstration of how such a generator is used.

Introducing the MySpace Profile Editor

When you stray from MySpace, founders Tom and Chris take notice. Because of this, they're eager to make sure your MySpace experience is fun and fulfilling so that people stick around. Therefore, with the boost in the number of third-party customization sites and tools available, they've responded by providing their own profile-editing tool, aptly named the MySpace Profile Editor. You'll find access to this tool (in its first-release beta version as of this writing) from your MySpace account maintenance page (see Figure 6.2).

Figure 6.2 MySpace offers a new customizing Profile Editor, accessible from this account page link.

INTRODUCING THE MySPACE PROFILE EDIT SCREEN

To get started, look at the basic concept put forth by MySpace that enables page owners to begin telling the community a bit about themselves. From the MySpace account page, click on the text link, *Edit Profile*, to access the Profile Edit screen (see Figure 6.3).

On the Profile Edit screen, you'll be prompted with a series of labeled text boxes to tell about yourself and your interests. For many newcomers, this is the place to begin getting into the

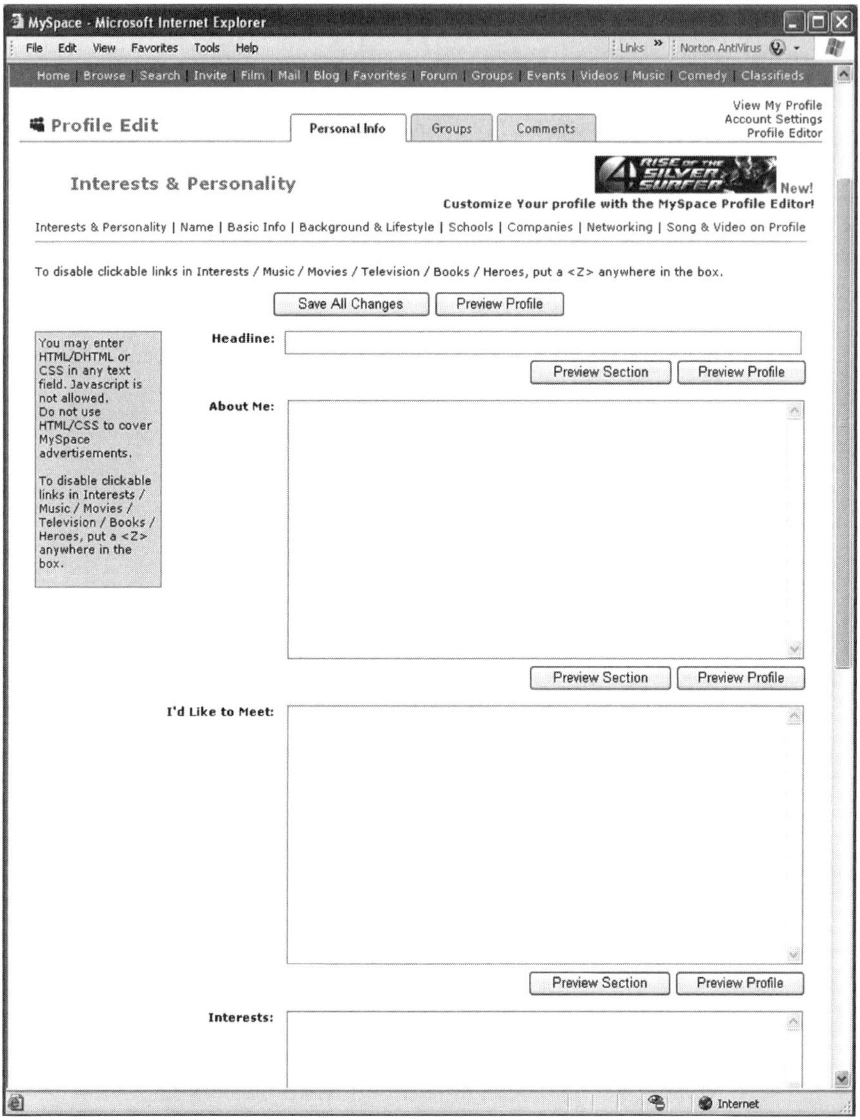

Figure 6.3 The MySpace Profile Editor gives you access to modify the various elements of the standard MySpace page as shown here.

groove of "sharing" themselves with the community. MySpace has given you a starting point by providing several text input boxes where you can tell about yourself, your interests, your favorite music, books, movies, and so on. If you simply wanted to provide this sort of information in a basic design layout, type away and save the changes to your profile by clicking on the *Save All Changes* button at the top of the screen. Of course, since this is a business-related page you're creating, you'll want to steer toward the business-centric information that will be of interest to your visitors, and you'll also want to customize the result so that it fits in with the overall design theme of your endeavor.

MySpace Tip

As you navigate into the different areas of profile customization and modification, there's always an easy way back to your main account page—the *Home* button. Notice the toolbar located near the top of the MySpace page (just under the main ad banner). Click on the *Home* button, and you'll immediately be back at your account main page where you can regain your bearings (see Figure 6.4).

Figure 6.4 If you get a bit lost while managing your MySpace profile, just click the *Home* text link on the page navigation bar to get back to your account maintenance home page.

GETTING STARTED WITH
CODE-BASED CUSTOMIZING

Even if you've never seen HTML or CSS code, you can still make good use of it in your MySpace profile without needing a programming background; if you can copy what you see here, you can use code. To prove it, try this simple exercise on your page. First, log in to your MySpace account and access the Edit Profile screen (refer to Figure 6.3). Now, within the About Me section, try entering something like this, using HTML:

<HTML>

<FONT SIZE=7 COLOR=PURPLE FACE=IMPACT>

Welcome to the DENCOMM page on MySpace.

</FONT>

</HTML>

Look at Figure 6.5 now to see what this looks like when typed (or copied) into the About Me section.

Before discussing the result of the HTML coding, take a look at the HTML tags in use. The tags are those instructions enclosed within the angle brackets (< >). The first tag you see, <HTML>, is the instruction that indicates that the following information is to be interpreted as HTML code. Next the FONT tag provides instructions on the display SIZE of the text, the COLOR of the text, and the FACE (that is, font or typeface and style) of the text. Those instructions, enclosed with the trailing angle bracket, tell the computer that the text line that follows, "Welcome to the DENCOMM page on MySpace," is to be presented with those font characteristics.

To see the effect of the HTML tagging, click on either the *Preview Section* button (to preview just the section where HTML is

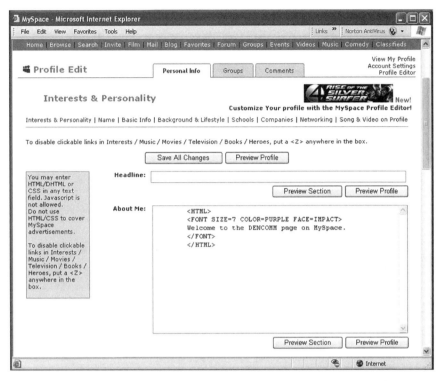

Figure 6.5 Using HTML code in your MySpace profile is as simple as typing text with special HTML formatting tags. Hey—you're coding!

entered) or the *Preview Profile* button (to preview the effect of the HTML in the overall layout of your MySpace page. Take a look at Figure 6.6 to see the effect of this simple piece of HTML tagging within my overall profile design.

As you can see in Figure 6.6, the HTML tags established prior to the actual text I wanted to include on my page has been formatted in a larger font, the Impact font style, and in an alternate color as specified. From this point, I can easily create additional text within the same About Me section, and I can change the text size, color, and typeface by using additional HTML tags to alter the subsequent text. Notice, though, that I first "closed" the tags I used in the previous example by establishing </FONT>. This closing tag indicates that the previous text characteristics initiated by the

Figure 6.6 Simple HTML tags can give different size, color, and style to the text you input on your MySpace page.

opening <FONT> tag are now complete and that those character-istics shouldn't apply to subsequent text. To create additional text with different characteristics, simply establish another <FONT> tag and then close that out with the </FONT> tag when that section is complete (notice that the forward slash [/] signifies a closing tag. When all HTML tagging is complete for a section you're modifying, be sure to establish the </HTML> tag to close the opening <HTML> tag.

MySpace Tip

If you're curious to experiment more with creating your own HTML, here are some of the most common tags you can practice with:

Font Tags

- <B>bold</B> results in **BOLD**.

- <I>italics</I> results in *ITALICS*

- <U>underline</U> results in UNDERLINE

- <FONT SIZE=12 COLOR=black FACE=comic sans> results in text THAT LOOKS LIKE THIS. This font will remain in use until you insert the </font> tag or specify another similar font equation with different settings.

Paragraphs, Line Breaks, and List Tags

- <P> will generate a paragraph break.

-
 will create a line break (similar to a carriage return).

- <LI> will generate a bullet mark before the text, as in a bulleted list.

Play around with creating customized blocks of text using these tags, making sure to preview the changes you make *before* you commit the changes to your profile.

When you get a result you like and would like to save the HTML coding to your profile, just click on the *Save All Changes* button at the top (or at the bottom) of the Edit Profile screen. The changes you made in any and all of the input sections will be written to your profile; you can build upon this content or change it whenever you like.

Choosing to Go with CSS

As you research more about the pages you see on MySpace (and consider contacting another user who has a page you particularly like and would like to learn how it was constructed), you'll discover that CSS is used prolifically to improve upon the abilities of HTML. CSS is similar to HTML in that you establish commands to apply to text and layouts, except the "tagging" is different (and, honestly, CSS is definitely more complex in its construction). However, the results are terrific and, in the end, CSS is an easier approach to achieving some great layouts that would have been tremendously cumbersome with HTML alone.

To give you an introduction to some basic CSS applications in your MySpace profile, take this example that enables you to remove the "extended network" banner that appears, by default, on all MySpace pages (and perhaps you feel having it there simply clashes with your design):

```
<style type="text/css">

table tbody td table tbody tr td.text table {visibility:hidden;}

table tbody td table tbody tr td.text table table, table tbody td
    table tbody tr td.text table table tbody td.text {visibility:
    visible;}

</style>
```

Simple, yes? Well, maybe not, although you should be able to detect the opening and closing tags that indicate this is CSS code. The intrinsic nature of the various table notations align with the overall MySpace design and, ultimately, target the "extended network" box and set it to "visibility:hidden." And this is just the bare beginning.

MySpace Tip

Because MySpace as been deemed the newest place where bad design runs rampant, some savvy MySpace users have determined the need to disable CSS-induced effects when they view others' pages. Using the Mozilla Firefox browser with the Web Developer extension enabled, CSS coding can be disabled while viewing an egregiously designed page. It doesn't affect the page's code; it just prevents the CSS enhancements from being displayed during the viewer's visit. To learn more about this, refer to the appendix for link details. Be sure to keep this in mind as you design your page, taking care not to overdo it lest your CSS efforts be disabled by those you hope to attract.

But if just looking at this CSS snippet (and the previous HTML example) causes you anxiety and makes you want to abandon any hope of designing a tasteful and effective MySpace page for your business, take heart. There is an easier way.

USING MySPACE PROFILE GENERATORS

As mention earlier in this chapter, there are a tremendous number of profile generators that will do all the complex customization coding for you, allowing you to easily modify your profile without getting your hands dirty or causing your head to hurt. And, although hard-core coders might pooh-pooh this approach as a sort of a beginner's crutch, the fact is that many of the generators available to you can render some excellent results that might serve your needs perfectly and save you time and effort in the process (and *that's* good business, by the way).

Again, there are numerous MySpace profile generators out there, and any Google search you do will provide you with pages of results. The task, then, is to wade through some of the lesser generators, those that are rife with ad space and pop-up and pop-under ad windows, and zero in on one or two that can give you what you need without polluting your computer screen. To get you started, here's a look at a couple of profile generators that I've found to be useful enough and that can establish a solid base of customization that you could, if you're so inclined, modify directly with CSS or HTML code going forward.

Freecodesource.com

One of the most streamlined profile generators I've found resides at Freecodesource.com (www.freecodesource.com), as shown in Figure 6.7.

This is a site that's all about MySpace, offering a variety of code generators and plenty of premade layouts you can use as a basis

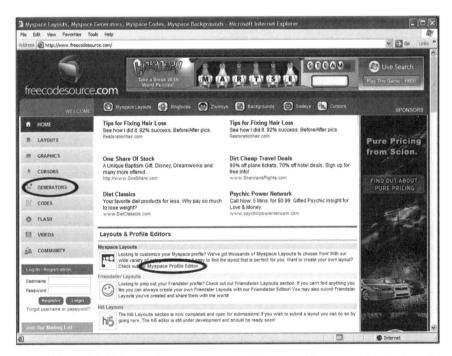

Figure 6.7 Visit www.freecodesource.com to access this company's robust profile generator.

for your own page, customizable however you'd like. Freecode source.com is somewhat ad-laden (this is how sites like these remain free), but it's not to an overwhelming effect. Visit the site to begin your simplified profile customization, clicking on either the *Generators* button or the *MySpace Profile Editor* text link from the home page (see Figure 6.8).

As you can see in Figure 6.8, the Freecodesource.com profile editor provides a very clean and well-organized tabular layout that allows you to intuitively customize the different elements of your MySpace page layout. You can easily specify color schemes, background and border settings, and font styles and sizes. Plus you are

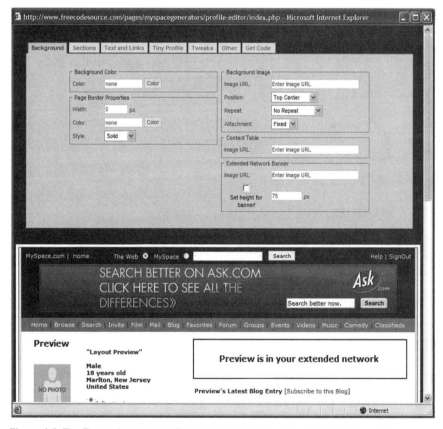

Figure 6.8 The Freecodesource profile generator allows you to immediately see the effect of the customizations you select.

able to utilize several "tweaks" in which you can suppress some of the standard layout elements that don't suit your design approach. The best feature of this particular third-party generator is the preview pane that allows you to immediately see the effect your customizations will have on your actual page (refer to the lower section of Figure 6.8). This way, you have a kind of sandbox where you can change settings as you choose until you get just the right look.

When you've arrived at a design that you think is suitable, simply click on the *Get Code* tab. The generator will then provide you with the HTML and CSS to achieve the layout on your MySpace page (see Figure 6.9). At this point, just click within the code window to highlight all the code text and copy it to your computer's clipboard (press CTRL-C on your keyboard). Now, log in and edit

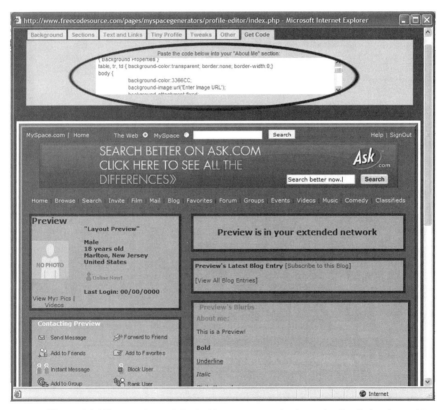

Figure 6.9 When you're satisfied with your customizations, the *Get Code* tab provides the code that you can cut and paste into your MySpace Profile Edit fields. How simple!

your MySpace profile and paste (CTRL-V on the keyboard or *Edit > Paste* from your Web browser's toolbar) into the About Me box within your MySpace Profile Edit screen. The field will be populated with the generated code and you can then click on the *Preview Profile* button to see how the code delivers within MySpace.

MySpace Tip

Because you've been given free use of the Freecodesource.com profile generator, expect to find some automatically inserted information that promotes the site. Look for the following code that will come along with the generated code:

```
</style><a href="http://www.freecodesource.com" style=
"position:absolute; top:0px;background-repeat:no-re-
peat;left:0px; height:155px; width:115px; background-
image:url(http://freecodesource.com/images/promote/c
lickhere.gif); background-position:left;"></a><br><br>
Layout Created @ FreeCodeSource.com <br> <a href=
"http://www.freecodesource.com"><b>Myspace Layouts
</b></a> <br> <a href="http://www.freecodesource.
com"><b>Myspace Codes</b></a> <br> <a href="http://
www.freecodesource.com"><b>Myspace Generators</b>
</a><br>
```

Essentially, this code will insert a flashing block at the top of your MySpace page that invites visitors to click on it and visit Freecodesource.com for themselves. Additionally, this code will insert link text into the About Me section of your layout, also encouraging your visitors to click on over to Freecodesource.com. If you don't want this content to be included in your profile, simply delete it from the rest of the generated code. If, however, you feel it is appropriate to help promote Freecodesouce.com for the help it has given you, leave this code as is.

A Look at the MySpace Profile Generator

Of course, the second profile generator worth mentioning here is MySpace's own design, created to help provide the community members with the tools they need within the MySpace realm. You can launch the editor by clicking on the text link within the Profile Edit page (see Figure 6.10).

You'll navigate to the Profile Editor (still in Beta version as of this writing) where you'll see a large *Start* button; click on it (see Figure 6.11).

Within the Profile Editor, you'll find a tab-organized layout where you can easily customize your page's background, modules, images, text, and links (see Figure 6.12). The changes you specify in

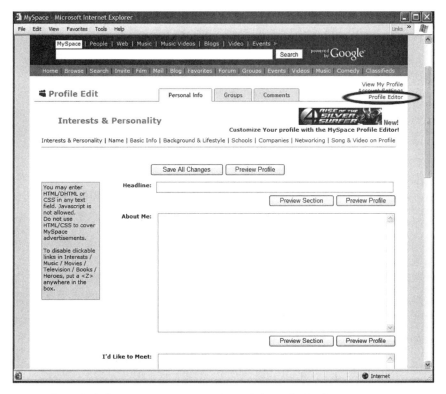

Figure 6.10 Click the text link to launch the MySpace Profile Generator.

Figure 6.11 On the MySpace Profile Editor screen, click on the *Start* button to begin customizing your page.

the settings on each tab will be visible on the sample display located below the tabs (similar to the Freecodesource.com generator). At any time, you can elect to save your customizations, undo or redo your work in progress, or clear the slate by choosing to restart.

When you're satisfied with the profile customizations you've made, click on the *Save* button, and MySpace will generate the code you need to apply the settings to your profile (see Figure 6.13). The difference in the MySpace code is that you'll paste this into the bottom of your Who I'd Like To Meet section on the Edit Profile page rather than in the "About Me" section (as was done with the Freecodesource-generated code). Just as easy as that, you have a customized profile.

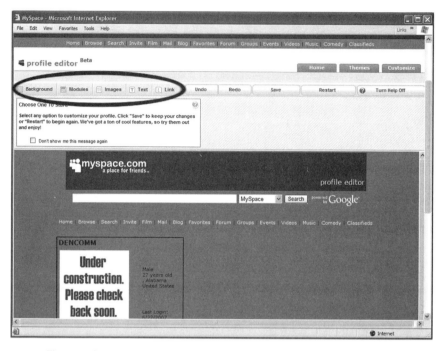

Figure 6.12 The MySpace Profile Editor also provides a what-you-see-is-what-you-get profile customization.

LOOKING BACK TO ASSESS THE STYLE

Now that you have a bit of a feel for the ways you can manipulate the look of your MySpace page and you've been enjoying messing around with colors, fonts, and so on, think again about the tenets of effective Web design. While it's true that you want and need to differentiate yourself within the burgeoning MySpace community, you don't want your page to emerge as a poster child for *When Web Designs Go Bad*. Therefore, see how well you're aligning with the guiding principles that make online content most memorable in the minds of those who experience it:

- *Background check*. Perhaps the most cited problem with Web page designs is the background. If you're going to use

Figure 6.13 The MySpace Profile Editor provides the code you need to apply the customizations you choose.

a background image, keep it static and consider making it semitransparent (to give it that faded sort of look) so that your blocks of text have contrast. If you're using a background texture, keep it easy on the eyes without too vibrant a color scheme and without starkly contrasting colors. When choosing a background color, consider one where your overall page will utilize similar or complementary colors or tones derived from the background.

- *Invasion of the incredibly obnoxious color combinations.* Red on green looks great on a Christmas tree but rarely on a

Web page. Watch out for teal blue on black backgrounds or any other color combinations that are glaring and garish. Eyestrain has become a top problem among avid Web surfers, and, these days, folks are ready to bail out the moment they encounter a page that incorporates color combinations that make the eyes bob and bounce.

- *Font frenzy.* In desktop publishing, the rule is simple: Don't use more than four fonts in any one publication. This carries over to Web design, specifically a MySpace page. Use your fonts sparingly or your page will look like a ransom note (unless that's the design you were looking for). Use the same font for all your headings and a consistent font for the content under those. Beware of using too many font sizes, too, and avoid significant differences between a heading font size and the subsequent content font size.

- *Connecting above the fold.* In Web design, "above the fold" refers to the information a reader will see immediately as if the page were a horizontally folded newspaper or brochure. You need to connect with your readers in the area above the fold so as not to lose their interest immediately. In an online application, this means you need to connect with the MySpace visitor before scrolling downward is required. Of course, even though you've seen the customizations you can make to the MySpace page layout in this chapter, it's still important to establish good information in the topmost sections of the page (including the Personal Info, About Me, and Blog Entry spaces). Good color and font designs definitely help make a visual connection, but compelling content is also required above the fold.

Remember that beauty is in the eye of the beholder, and one person's mess might be another person's masterpiece. In the end, the design you bestow upon your page (and those who visit it) is purely one of personal taste—yours. Do what seems best to fulfill the needs of your overall plan, but be ready to make adjustments if your original lime green and sherbet orange pattern doesn't seem to be going over too well.

GO EASY, OR THEY'LL GO AWAY

As fun as it is to customize your page, loading it up with all sorts of great images, multimedia content, and so on, just remember that the more you cram onto that front page, the longer it will take to display. This means that your visitors will need to wait (and wait and wait?) for all that nifty stuff to load before they can marvel at your handiwork—and many *won't* wait. If your page takes longer than, say, 15 seconds to load, you might as well forget about it; visitors will bolt before your terrific design is fully displayed. For example, one page I particular admire is that of Doombuggies at www.myspace.com/doombuggies (see Figure 6.14). This is a cleverly crafted page that is devoted to the classic Disney park attraction The Haunted Mansion (and "doom buggies" are those egglike cars you sit in as you tour the ghostly goings-on).

The Doombuggies page is full of great material, and it wisely provides directions to the actual Web site, www.doombuggies.com, to further entice visitors. However, the MySpace page sometimes takes up to 20 seconds or more to load (depending upon the speed of the connection). Without question, it's worth the wait to those who like the attraction, but passersby might continue on their way rather than wait. Be sure to test your MySpace page constantly to be sure your great design won't be left unnoticed by the less patient among us (and try to display your page design on as many differ-ent computers as possible—at home, at work, at a library, at a friend's home—to see how long it takes to download on different computers and with different Internet connections).

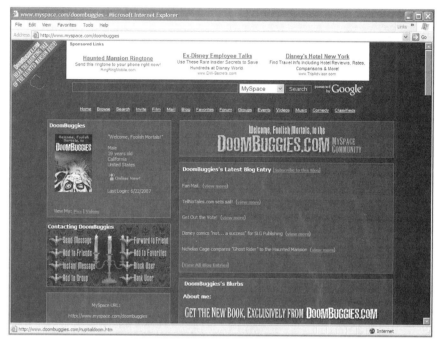

Figure 6.14 The Doombuggies page at MySpace is terrific fun but, much like the actual Disney attraction it celebrates, you might have to wait a bit before you can board the ride.

WHAT YOU CAN'T (OR SHOULDN'T) CUSTOMIZE AT MySPACE

Last but not least, make sure that you're fully aware of the page elements that MySpace deems as inalterable, specifically mentioned in the terms of use agreement you accepted when you created your account. Don't worry—there's nothing here with teeth or anything particularly draconian; just be aware that MySpace needs to pay its bills and, therefore, insists that you not use code to mask or otherwise eliminate the header ad banners you see atop each MySpace page (with exceptions going to major companies and other big players who recompense the site for this privilege).

At this time, MySpace is an open design realm, and it's fully possible for individuals to override the site's banner ads and modify other key elements that are earmarks of a MySpace page. Any page that has done this is subject to deletion, so you'll need to determine if you're willing to take that risk, especially after the work you've done to establish a fetching page design. It's easy to create a great page while still staying within this minor boundary MySpace has stated. Play by the rules, and you'll reap the benefits of the MySpace experience.

With that done, it's time to put an even more personal stamp on your page—*you!* With colors and fonts understood, move ahead to Chapter 7 now to begin sharing your smiling face, your favorite music, and your best-loved videos with the rest of the community. You'll quickly find that adding these key pieces of personality will do wonders for your page, your visitor rate, and your business.

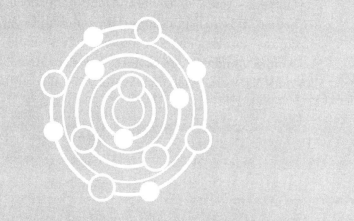

ADDING
PICTURES, MUSIC,
AND VIDEO TO
YOUR PAGE

N ow that you have some style infused into your MySpace page, it's time to "get with the picture," if you will. Another big draw of the MySpace experience is the opportunity for community members to post and share personal things and information about themselves, namely media. In its purest sense, social networking is founded on sharing not only written information about oneself but also sharing photos as well as including favorite songs and videos. To this end, the experience morphs into something resembling

a personal broadcasting studio (and, as a youngster, didn't you sometimes fantasize about what music you'd play if you were in charge
of the radio station or what shows you'd play if you were at the
controls of the local TV station?).

MySpace makes it easy to round out the "snapshot" of who
you are and what you like by allowing you to add these kinds
of multimedia elements to your profile. And, from a business
standpoint, this is your opportunity to achieve several feats that
will draw in your clientele (or audience) in a way that is easy
and immediate.

MAKING THE MOST OF THE MEDIA

Again, before jumping into uploading fever and cramming your
MySpace page with everything and anything you can conjure up,
give some thought to the purpose and intended result of your page.
In some cases, uploading the media becomes a foregone conclusion if the page owner and operator will rely on the content to
attract visitors (as when a band posts songs, a filmmaker posts
short films, or a photographer posts images of his or her work). If
your market niche isn't so cut and dried with respect to the sort
of media you should post, take a moment to consider the best
approach.

For example, if you're operating a metropolitan coffeehouse,
you likely wouldn't post photos of your coffee beans or upload a
video of how you steam a latte (then again, maybe there's a clever
opportunity here). Perhaps you'd post images of your coffeehouse,
from the inviting storefront with the quaint bistro tables and stylish
awnings to the cozy interior that shows your patrons enjoying a
superb cup of java. If you feature particular styles of music at you
shop—jazz, lounge, new age, or whatever—perhaps you might
post a music clip so that your page exudes the same atmosphere
your visitors would encounter *if they were actually there*. And, if

you feature live performances of any sort on a quaint stage in the corner, post some video clips of that so that potential visitors can see what awaits them when they pay a visit to your shop.

You get the idea—this all serves as more mood and tone setting in a way that promotes your business goals while providing a virtual tour of your establishment. Unfortunately, MySpace doesn't yet have a means to deliver *aroma* through its interface so you won't be able to tempt your online patrons with the rich smell of your superlative coffee beans (but some well-composed photos of a steamy cup of coffee with an accompanying pastry might do the trick just as well).

The point is this: Think about the sights and sounds that will trigger a positive reaction in your visitors so that they'll be practically compelled to visit your brick-and-mortar business or venture over to your commercial Web site to find out more about what it is you offer.

MySpace Tip

And if you're interested in doing further research into the ways and means of effective product marketing and corralling consumer attitudes, check out the appendix for details about two excellent books, *Why We Buy: The Science of Shopping* by Paco Underhill and *The Tipping Point: How Little Things Can Make a Big Difference* by Malcolm Gladwell.

More Ideas for Photos to Serve Your Space's Purpose

The coffeehouse example is rather specific, so here are some additional tips for the sorts of images that might work well within different kinds of MySpace page settings. From a business perspective, photos can serve as a catalog of products and services and more. Here are a few ideas of how photos can be used from a businessperson's perspective:

Musicians

- Official portraits of the musician(s)

- Photos from a recent performance (or any performance)

- Images of CDs or DVDs of performances

- Images of other official merchandise

Service Providers (Craftspeople, Artists, Home Improvements, etc.)

- Images of the tools used to render services

- Images of the results of the services

Writers

- Official press photo of the writer

- Images of book covers

- Images of article publications (digital renderings of "clippings")

- Photos from appearances (book signings, talks, media events)

Resellers

- Photo of the seller

- Photos of items for sale (though they won't be for sale directly on MySpace)

- Photos of a brick-and-mortar store, if applicable

That should be enough discussion to get your own thoughts in motion regarding the sort of photos that would be appropriate for your business's MySpace page. Don't be afraid to add some personal photos, too, but just be certain they uphold your business persona and don't serve as a distraction (or embarrassment!) to your efforts.

Technical Matters: Photo File Types and Sizing for Success

Before you go about uploading photos, you first need to prepare the images. While many images you have will upload just fine, it's important to know that MySpace imposes a restriction upon the size of the pictures you can post—they must be no larger than 5 megabytes (MB) each and must be in .gif or .jpg format. To avoid any hassles in the uploading process, take MySpace's advice to size and format your photos before you attempt to show them off.

Photo File Formats

As already mentioned, MySpace limits you to utilizing .gif and .jpg file formats for any photos you wish to upload to your profile. Generally, this won't put any undue limitation upon you since these are the most common file types for photographic files. If you have a photo you want to use that's in a different format (such as a TIFF [.tif] or PhotoShop [.psd] format), you'll need to open these with the appropriate computer application and resave them as either a .gif or .jpg file. But is one file format better than another? The answer to that depends upon the content of the photo. Here are a couple of quick tips on which format to use:

- A .gif file can display up to only 256 colors (very few by digital imaging standards) and are best suited to images with few colors, black and white images, or nonphotographic images or logos.

- A .jpg file can render up to 16 million colors and is the best choice for a very colorful and detailed photograph.

Size While You Shoot (or Scan)

With the file format understood, now it's important to have your images properly sized before you attempt to upload them to MySpace. If you want to show off the photos you've taken yourself, the easiest way to size them is to modify the image quality within your digital camera. Even though today's cameras boast incredible 8+ megapixel resolutions, this will render an image too large for MySpace. If you simply wish to share a photo of general interest, select a lower-quality setting on your camera *before* you take the picture. The quality of your image will still be great (recall the days not so very long ago when 2.1 megapixels was astounding?) and you'll have a photo that's ready to upload the moment you've taken it.

The same holds true if you'll be scanning photos to create digital equivalents to upload to your MySpace page. When you scan specifically for MySpace use, select a dpi (dots per inch) setting of 72. Yes, this is a lower-quality resolution, but the results should still suit your purposes just fine.

Finally, if you want to upload images that are preexisting and which exceed MySpace's size constraints, simply open the files within an appropriate computer application and shrink down the image (you can usually do this by selecting the image and dragging inward a "rubber band" border around the image). When the image has been properly shrunk, you simply resave the photo. To double-check to see if the resized photo is within the 5MB limit, simply right-click on the file name within your file manager program and select "Properties" to access the file details including its size (see Figure 7.1)

Resizing Large Photos

Thankfully, MySpace suggests a photo resizing tool that will address the issue of resizing large photos cleanly and easily—IrfanView.

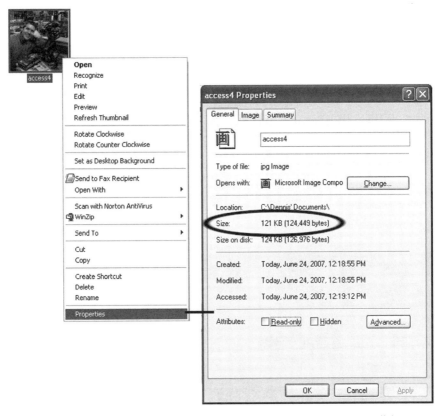

Figure 7.1 To check the size of an image you want to upload to MySpace, right-click on the file and check the size value. Here, the reported 121 kilobytes is well below the 5MB limit.

MySpace Tip

What if it's important that your visitors (that is, customers or clientele) be able to inspect very large and very detailed images of what you want to share? There's no getting around the MySpace image size restriction, but consider adding an active link to your own Web site where the larger images can be inspected. To make this opportunity clear to your visitors, add text to the images that encourages lookers to visit the link to take an even closer look.

UPLOADING IMAGES AND CREATING PHOTO ALBUMS

With your images ready, it's time to upload them to your MySpace profile. Begin by uploading the image that will serve as your *default profile image* (recall from Chapter 4 that I chose to upload an "under construction" image when I created my account). To begin uploading a default image, log in to your MySpace account and click on the *Add/Edit Photos* text link (see Figure 7.2).

Figure 7.2 Click on the *Add/Edit Photos* link to begin uploading images to your MySpace account.

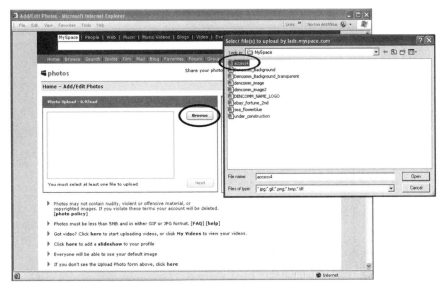

Figure 7.3 Click on *Browse* to select the image file on your computer and upload it to your MySpace profile.

When you click on the link, you'll navigate to the photos page where you'll find a Photo Upload box and a *Browse* button; click on *Browse* to locate the image file you want to upload from your computer (see Figure 7.3).

After you've selected the image file from your computer, click on the *Open* button on the file box, and the file will be captured within the MySpace Photo Upload box; click on the *Next* button. This navigates you forward to select an *album* for your photo. Albums on MySpace act like file folders for your images. Consider logical groupings for the photos you'll upload and create albums accordingly, such as "Our Store," "Menu Items," and "Featured Acts" (to recall the coffee house example). For now, I'll simple use the suggested default album, "My Photos." Click on the *Upload* button to continue, and MySpace will show you the status of the upload process. Refer to Figure 7.4 to review these three steps to select and upload a photo. Click on *Next* to continue.

On the subsequent screen, MySpace will display a thumbnail version of your uploaded image and allow you to type in a caption

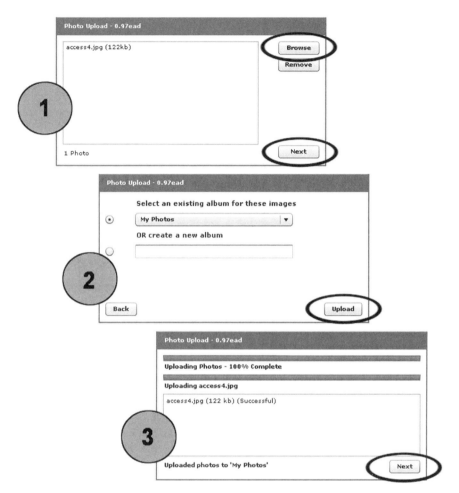

Figure 7.4 Uploading a photo to your MySpace profile is as easy as 1-2-3.

for it (captions are displayed underneath the image within your photo album; this is a great place to include either a description of the image or a URL that will enable folks to view a larger-sized version on your Web site). If you enter a caption, click on the *Save* button when you're done. But if you don't want to provide a caption, simply click on the *Skip this Step* button to proceed (see Figure 7.5)

Next you'll see the contents of your photo album, as shown in Figure 7.6. At this point, notice that below the "under construction" image is an asterisk which notes that the image shown is the current default image; it's time to replace that. The *Set as Default*

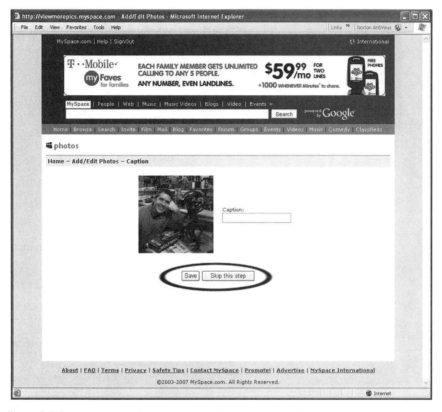

Figure 7.5 Review the uploaded image, and add a caption if you like.

button located below my newly uploaded image will set this as the main image shown on my profile page.

MySpace Tip

Incidentally, if you have a temporary default image (as I had) or simply want to clean up your photo album a bit, click on the *Edit* button under any existing image where you can access a new screen to move the photo to a new or existing photo album, create or edit a caption, or delete the image entirely.

And, like that, you've updated your default image, the one visitors will see when they drop by your page (see Figure 7.7). From

Figure 7.6 With a new photo uploaded, simply click on the *Set as Default* button to establish the image as your default photo.

here, you can continue to upload additional photos to your MySpace albums as you see fit. And while there is the 6MB restriction on the size of each image, you'll be happy to know that there's currently no limit to the number of images you can upload and maintain with your MySpace account. Enjoy!

UPLOADING AUDIO AND VIDEO FILES

Next up, let's add some multimedia to the profile to give it more appeal to visitors and give them an excuse to hang around a bit and

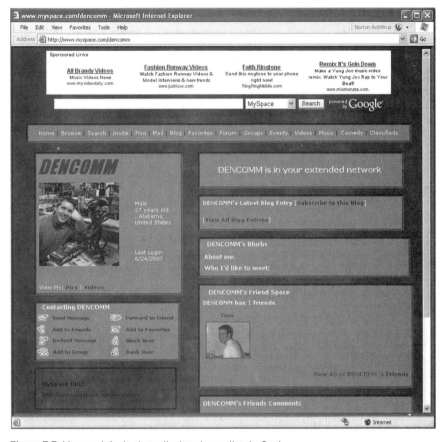

Figure 7.7 My new default photo displays immediately. Cool.

browse while they listen to a song or watch a quick video. Perhaps you remember the terms of use agreement when you created your account; the content on your MySpace page must never infringe upon the copyrights of others. While that's true, the great news is that many recording artists, filmmakers, and other copyright holders maintain their own MySpace pages and have content that they're eager to share, essentially inviting you to post their stuff on your page.

By including their owned content, they also agree to let MySpace community members include it in their profiles without infringement (and the fact is that a song or film clip shared across the MySpace community means free advertising to the copyright holder). With that settled, begin by adding a song to your profile. You can do this by searching for an artist directly within MySpace and, chances are, you'll find him, her, or them.

For example, since my default image pictures me flanked by an assortment of pop culture collectibles, I'll seek out something vintage—Cheap Trick. The band that rocked Japan's Budokan arena some several decades ago is still at it and has a MySpace page too. I hopped over to that page and found that the jukebox contained several choice cuts. I decided to add one of the shared songs to my profile; it was easy. First, users with a music profile can host a jukebox of songs on MySpace (see Figure 7.8).

I located a song I liked and simply clicked on the *Add* link next to the song. Upon doing so, MySpace prompted me to confirm that I wanted to add the selected song to my own profile. When you want to add a song to your profile, click on the *Add Song to Profile*

Figure 7.8 When you find a song you want to use to greet your visitors, simply click on *Add* to include it on your profile.

Figure 7.9 Click on the button to confirm the addition of the song to your profile.

button to proceed, and MySpace will provide the results of your addition (see Figure 7.9).

With a song added to your MySpace profile, the media player will be displayed on your MySpace page where visitors can click on the *play* button and give a listen (see Figure 7.10).

Also, if you decide that you want to have the song launch automatically when a visitor views your page, return to the My Account Settings screen and click on the Music Settings text link where you can uncheck the auto-play disable box (see Figure 7.11).

MySpace Tip

Consider changing your profile song from time to time just to keep things interesting. If you do not have a music profile, you can have only one song linked to your profile at a time. Musicians can establish a jukebox like the one I linked from within the Cheap Trick page.

On the video side, linking video files is done very much the same way as linking music files. From the MySpace home page, you can begin searching for video content within the community

Figure 7.10 In just a couple of clicks, you can have a music player on your page.

by clicking on the *Videos* link on the topmost navigation bar and entering search keywords. When you find a video you like, you can view it using the MySpace video player, and you can easily add it to your MySpace page by clicking on either the Add to My Profile text link to display it on your home page or the Add to My Favorites to link it in the Videos section of your profile (see Figure 7.12).

If you click on the Add to My Profile text link, the video will be immediately added to your home page display without the need for confirmation steps (see Figure 7.13).

Just as with music files, you can display only a single video file at a time on your MySpace home page; you can add as many videos as you like to the My Favorites area of your profile. Of course, MySpace isn't the only place to find video files, most folks are quite aware of

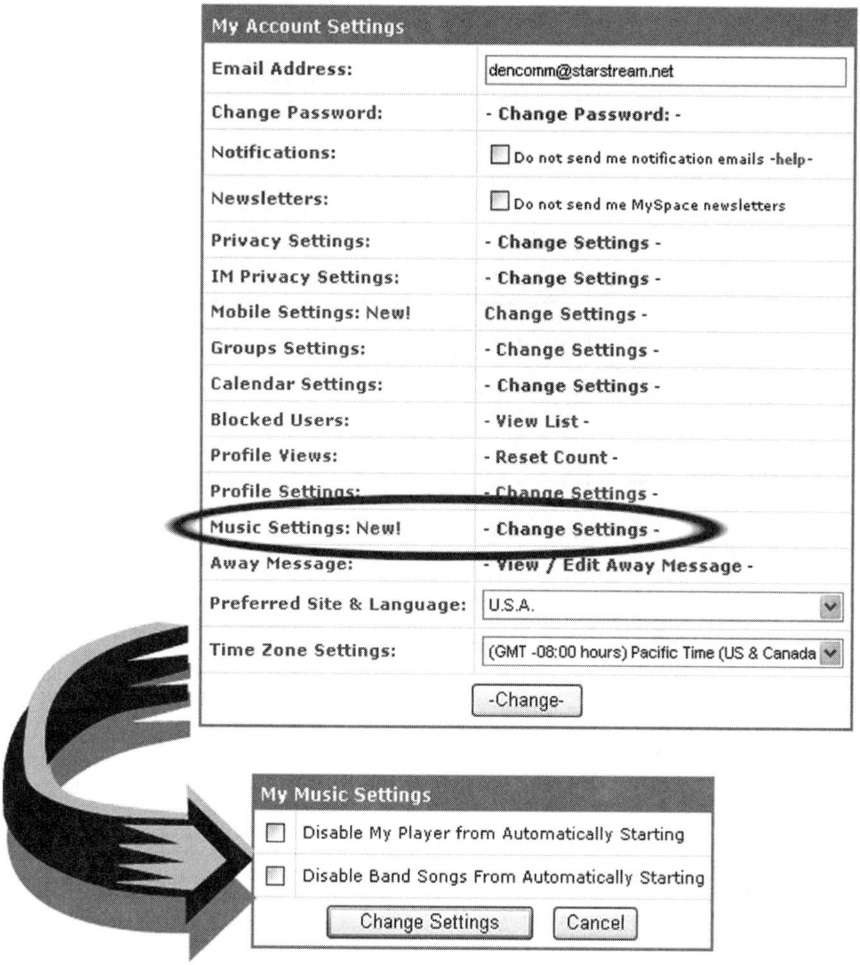

Figure 7.11 Revisit your profile settings to change whether songs will automatically play when visitors drop by your page.

the content available at YouTube (www.youtube.com) and Google Video (http://video.google.com). You can search either of those sites for additional video content you might wish to include in your profile, copying in the reference URLs plus some handy sizing HTML to get the video to display nicely on your page. For example:

<object type="application/x-shockwave-flash" allowScript Access ="never" allowNetworking="internal" height="350" width = "425" data="http://www.youtube.com/v/NeBUMYG-iP4">

Figure 7.12 Within MySpace, search for video content and add it to your profile or favorites with the click of a button.

<param name="allowScriptAccess" value="never" />

<param name="allowNetworking" value="internal" />

<param name="movie" value="http://www.youtube.com/v / NeBUMYG-iP4" />

</object>

This code was copied into the "I'd Like To Meet" section of my profile, just below the customization code I pasted from the MySpace Profile Editor. The result can be seen in Figure 7.14.

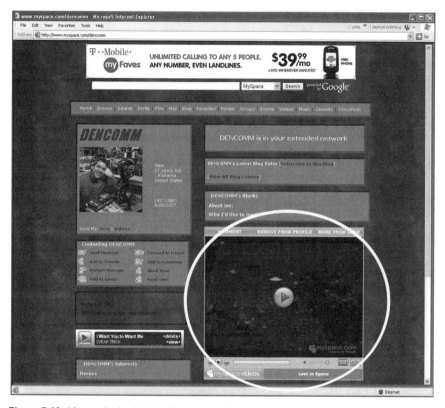

Figure 7.13 After a single click, I added a video file to my page.

Of course, you can add more videos to your MySpace profile without overstuffing your front page (a bad idea, really, since additional embedded video links can significantly increase the load time of your page).

USING MUSIC AND VIDEO TO PROMOTE YOUR PROFILE

So now your page is shaping up nicely, and you're establishing a real sense of what you and your business are all about. That said, how does it help you to link other folks' songs and video content if

Figure 7.14 Using HTML code pasted into my profile, I can easily add more videos to my home page at MySpace.

you're not the original creator? The content you link further establishes the tone and atmosphere of your business, and those audio and video files further define who you are and to whom you actively cater. If you're all about nostalgia and pop culture and collectibles and such (as I am), then it makes sense to include this sort of content to entertain your visitors while keeping within the realm of your overall business intent. Since I happen to actively write about film, television, and collectibles, my page is shaping up well to communicate that to my visitors. As it stands at this point, it seems a bit like a personal page rather than a business page, but I address that matter in the coming chapters.

ANNOUNCING
YOUR ARRIVAL
AND CHOOSING
YOUR FRIENDS—
WISELY

So here you are, ready to announce your grand opening and cheerfully greet all who come to visit you in your new place. This is the time when the social networking swings into high gear, and you begin the "friending" exercise to invite new visitors to come see you and pay repeat visits. For those who manage personal pages at MySpace, this is the crux of the experience—meeting and interacting with others who have similar interests (and even disinterests). For a business venture, here's where you begin to parade your wares—whatever they may be—in a way that will encourage folks to stop by for a look and hopefully tell their friends about the fun place you've got going.

In this chapter, then, you'll learn how to "friend" on MySpace (yes, it's a verb in this context) and how to become a friend to others. You'll learn how to search out community members with complementary interests and how to leverage their collection of friends, too. You'll also learn how to screen out some of the riffraff on MySpace to ensure that you're not wasting time and effort on those who might not be "true friends" to you or your business. Here's where it gets interesting as you now delve into the heart of what makes MySpace tick.

UNDERSTANDING THE ESSENCE OF THE "FRIEND REQUEST"

Although it may feel a bit uncomfortable and perhaps even unconventional to reach out to a stranger online and ask, "Can I be your friend?" the fact is that this is what's expected on MySpace. The other Spacers are doing the same and are expecting as much from you. The friending process is what makes MySpace the thriving community it is and, with respect to your business goals, it's the next step to take to help spread the word about you and your offerings. Friending is easy, fun, and even fascinating to behold as the virtual community buzzes about you, and you begin buzzing along with it.

FIRST STEP: COMPLETING THE REGISTRATION CONFIRMATION

Recall from Chapter 4, during the registration process, that MySpace had sent an e-mail message to the e-mail address you provided when you created your account. If you haven't opened that message

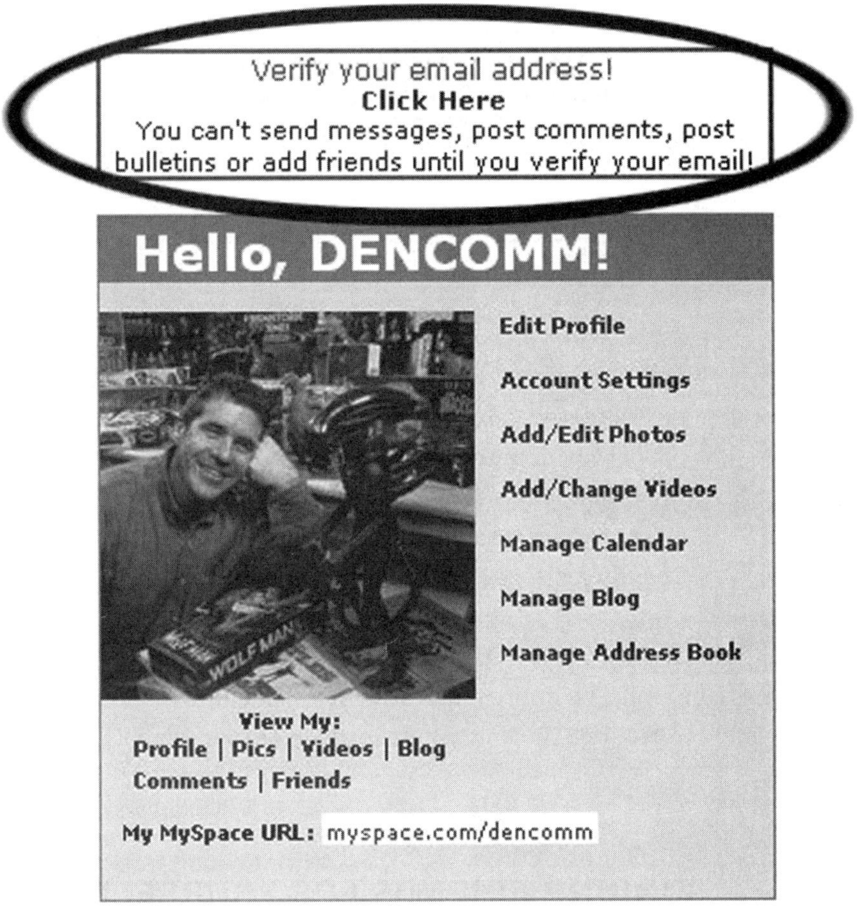

Figure 8.1 Until you respond to the verification e-mail message sent by MySpace to your specified e-mail account, you'll be unable to begin friending other Spacers.

to complete the registration process then, now's the time. Until you verify your e-mail address, a red-bordered box will appear on your MySpace main account page urging you to complete the process in order to enable the rest of the MySpace services (see Figure 8.1).

The e-mail message's intent is to confirm that the e-mail address you provided is valid and belongs to a "real person" rather than some programmatically generated bot designed to created MySpace accounts for whatever reason (likely spam or other such ignoble purposes). Within the e-mail address is a verification link that, when clicked on, will confirm that the message sent from MySpace reached an active e-mail account managed by a real person—you.

MySpace Tip

> If you cannot find or accidentally deleted the MySpace e-mail message, simply click on the *Click Here* text link within the red-bordered box on your main account page; that will enable you to request that the e-mail message be resent to the e-mail address you've specified (even to a new e-mail address if you modified that in your profile as I did during the Chapter 6 discussion).

Upon clicking the link embedded in the verification e-mail message, you'll be notified that your account confirmation is complete (see Figure 8.2). Now you're ready to get *friending*.

FINDING FRIENDS FOR YOURSELF

If there's something business owners are most anxious about, it's opening their doors and waiting for someone to show up. Many have grand notions that the locals have been waiting eagerly for the great new business place to open up, lining up around the block on the day heralded as the grand opening. Maybe that happens, but maybe it doesn't. At MySpace, while you were busy inside your virtual shop dressing the walls and preparing the initial content, you might have begun to imagine how many folks would be beating a path to your virtual door when you finally removed the Friends Only window blinds and began entertaining guests. Maybe that will happen; maybe it won't.

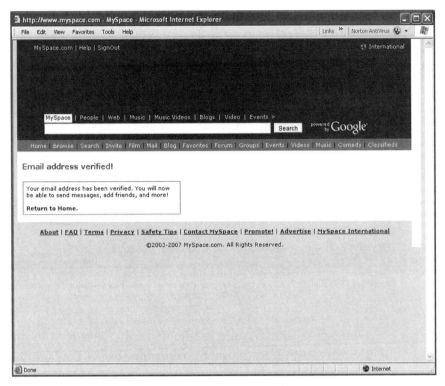

Figure 8.2 Your registration steps are now complete, and it's time to go get some friends.

The good news is that, at MySpace, if folks haven't yet found you, you can find *them*. Just as some might stand outside a brick-and-mortar business and hand out promotional handbills, you can walk the virtual neighborhood at MySpace to introduce yourself and your business to potential new friends.

Browsing for Buddies

Although this may feel like exploiting others, the fact is that MySpace is all about connecting with others who share your interests and can help you get more from your MySpace experience. This starts with browsing for others who are like-minded or who can be beneficial in helping you spread the word about your space.

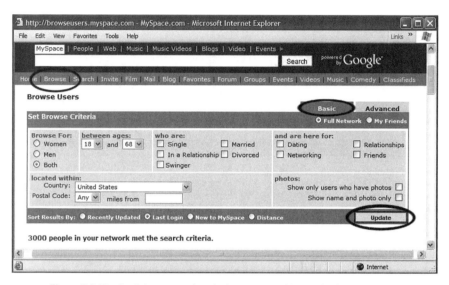

Figure 8.3 The Basic browse options help you get a wide swath of community members.

Therefore, from your account profile home page simply click on the Browse text link in the main navigation bar. When you do, you'll invoke the MySpace Browseusers screen showing the basic browse options (see Figure 8.3).

But browsing MySpace using the Basic browse selections simply won't yield the list of folks you'd be most interested in friending. Click on the *Advanced* tab on the Browseusers screen to access the full assortment of browse selection parameters, as shown in Figure 8.4.

Use the various check boxes, radio buttons, and pull-down selectors to enter browse parameters that you feel will best yield a list of useful potential friends. Also be sure to select the radio button that will run the browse request against the full network of MySpace users (and later, once you have established a collection of friends, you can browse among just those folks if you wish to further segment your associations). Click on the *Update* button at the bottom of the screen to initiate the browse and begin viewing the profiles of those community members who match your browse criteria.

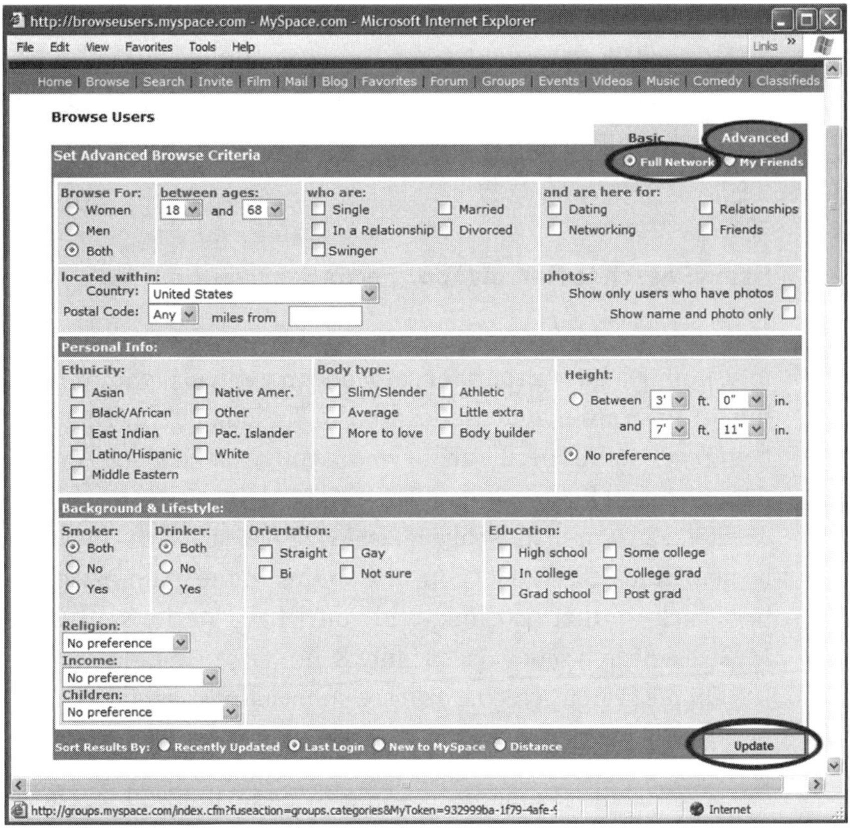

Figure 8.4 Using the Advanced tab on the Browseusers screen will yield a more refined result of potential friends for your page.

MySpace Tip

Having made the various selections in your browse, this becomes a good time to consider updating or modifying your *own* profile settings to ensure that they properly and accurately represent your page and purpose. Recall from Chapter 4 when you entered some basic information during account registration, including your home town, birth date, and so on. While it was fine to build your site with "unmaintained" information, now is a good time to revisit your profile—click on *Edit*

Profile and visit the "Basic Info," "Background & Lifestyle," and "Networking" areas—and adjust the information as it best suits you and your business presentation. Modify the information now, because you never know who might be browsing for *you.*

Using Search to Narrow Your Focus

Browsing the MySpace community for friends could be likened to scanning a busy airport for someone in particular without holding up a placard that identifies who you're looking for. Therefore, being even more specific about whom you're looking for—even by name—might help you zero in on the first friends you might wish to extend a warm handshake to. In MySpace, you can achieve this by using the Search selection, also found on the main navigation bar. Click on that text link, and you'll navigate forward to the MySpace Search screen (see Figure 8.5).

On the search screen, you'll see subheadings as follows:

- *Find a Friend.* Here you can search the MySpace profile information, same as you provided when you registered or modified your account setting, to locate particular MySpace members by their account Name, by their established Display Name (mine's Dencomm), or by their Email address. This is most useful for locating a personal friend but also for seeking out publicly known individuals such as actors, musicians, artisans, and so on (just beware that a page that bears your favorite singer might not be an "official" page operated by the singer himself or herself).

- *Classmate Finder.* Beyond looking to reconnect to reminisce about school days gone by, this is a great search tool for finding an entire student body, especially if the shared campus experience or the age demographic of these folks would suit your business offering.

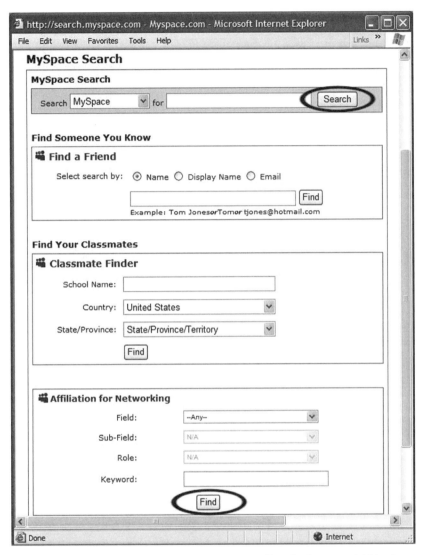

Figure 8.5 Using the MySpace Search screen helps you sift and select potential friends based upon their name, interests, and even school.

- *Affiliation for Networking.* If you're looking for other folks who do business in similar circles or provide the sorts of products and services you need to expand your potential, use this section to locate the sorts of people that would partner well with you and your business.

MySpace Search

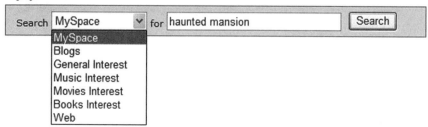

Figure 8.6 For best results in locating your target audience and associates, search MySpace with key words.

Once you enter search criteria in any of the above areas, simply click on the *Find* button at the bottom of the MySpace Search screen.

I deliberately withheld discussion of the other search field found on the MySpace Search screen, that top-most shaded area that allows you to search all of MySpace (or selected segments thereof) with general key words (see Figure 8.6).

My search for "haunted mansion" within MySpace, led me to the user, Doombuggies, noted in Chapter 6. In addition to that page, I found several other pages where users had developed their tributes to the long-loved Disney attraction. For my purposes and within the realm of analyzing and writing about pop culture, any and many of the pages I found from this search might make good friends. Search for whatever comes to mind that suits your page's intent, and see what friends might be awaiting you.

REACHING OUT AND MAKING
A FRIEND REQUEST

Don't be bashful—ask someone to be your friend. Remember, the MySpace community expects to hear from folks like you who are looking for friends, and members are eager to learn what you bring to the party. Since I have admired the Doombuggies page design and content (despite the slightly longish load time), I'll knock on the door and ask, "Will you be my friend?" Here's how:

1. Visit the MySpace page that interests you and is hosted by a person you'd like to befriend.

2. Click on the Add to Friends link within the page's Contacting box (see Figure 8.7).

3. MySpace will provide a confirmation pop-up window to be certain that you intended to add the profile page (and its owner) to your friends list. Click on the *Add to Friends* button to continue; click on the *Cancel* button if you've changed your mind (see Figure 8.8).

4. Upon clicking on *Add to Friends,* MySpace will let you know that an e-mail has been sent to the friend you'd like to add (refer to Figure 8.8), allowing that person to decide to accept or reject your request.

Figure 8.7 Locate the Contacting box on any MySpace user's page, and use the *Add to Friends* text link to make a new friend.

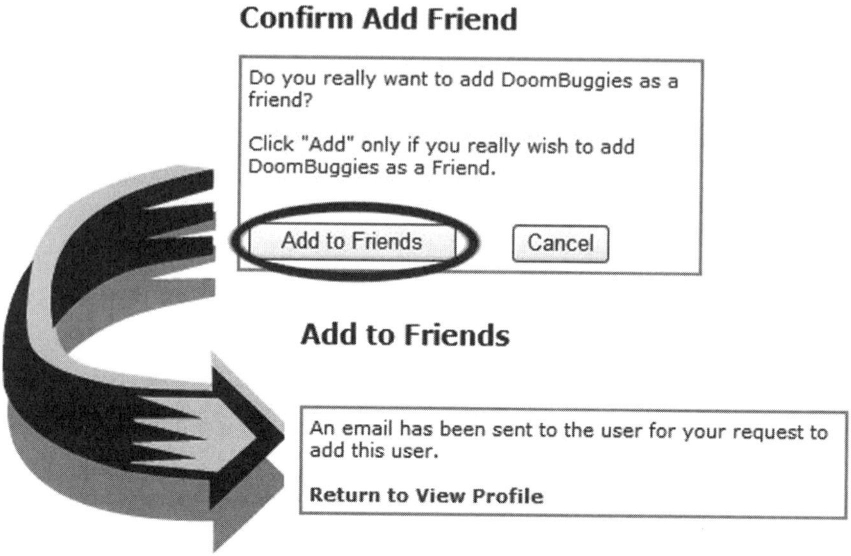

Confirm Add Friend

Do you really want to add DoomBuggies as a friend?

Click "Add" only if you really wish to add DoomBuggies as a Friend.

Add to Friends   Cancel

Add to Friends

An email has been sent to the user for your request to add this user.

Return to View Profile

Figure 8.8 Click on the *Add to Friends* button to initiate a friend request. MySpace will send an e-mail to the user to inform that person that you'd like to be his or her friend.

Now, you wait to see if the person you reached out to will accept your friend request. If so, he or she will be added to your Friend Space and you'll be added to his or hers. Until that happens, go ahead and seek out some other folks you'd like to have as friends.

Tracking Your Friend Requests

While you should never feel personally slighted if your friend request hasn't been immediately acknowledged, you can keep an eye on how your requests are faring. Simply revisit your MySpace account page and locate the My Mail box on the page. Then, click on the "friend requests" text link within the box and select the "Pending Request" text link thereafter (see Figure 8.9). This will gain you access to the status of your pending friend requests.

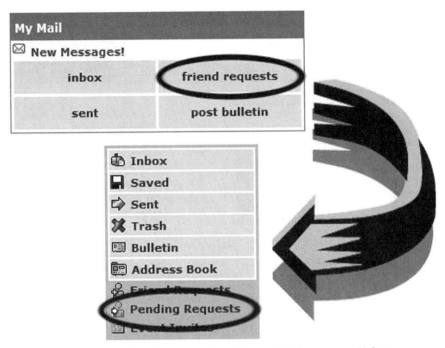

Figure 8.9 Click on the Friend Requests link within My Mail box on your MySpace maintenance page; then click on *Pending Requests* to check status of your friend requests.

Again, no need to worry if you find that some friend requests are still pending; some folks out there simply don't monitor their MySpace accounts 24 hours a day. Have faith, though, that they'll notice your request and will respond. If, however, you have a pending request and wish to withdraw it, you can do so by clicking on the *Cancel Request* button. On the other hand, if you think your friend request has somehow gone unnoticed, you can send a follow-up message by clicking on the *Send Message* button and reminding the recipient that you'd like to be that person's friend (see Figure 8.10).

Once your friend request has been accepted, you'll find that you have a new friend link in the My Friend Space of your profile (see how Doombuggies has become my new friend as shown in Figure 8.11).

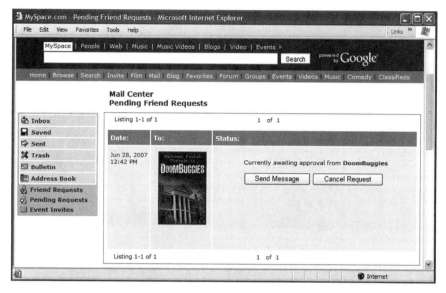

Figure 8.10 Pending friend requests will show as such and will provide you with an option to either cancel the request or to follow up with a Send Message reminder.

Figure 8.11 When a friend request is accepted, you'll find that you have a new friend in the My Friend Space area of your account.

RESPONDING TO FRIEND
REQUESTS YOU RECEIVE

At the same time you're sending friend requests to community members, others will begin noticing your page and will start sending friend requests to you. This is the reciprocal nature of MySpace, and you should expect to entertain and accept friend requests sent your way. When someone sends a friend request to you (and you'll hope, for your business's sake that there will be many), you'll receive an e-mail notification that a Spacer has asked to become your friend. You can either respond to the request directly within the e-mail message (there's a link that will navigate you to the appropriate area of your MySpace account), or you can visit your MySpace account home page and review the My Mail box again, this time noticing the + *New Friends Requests!* link (see Figure 8.12). Click on that link to access the *Mail Center Friend Request Manager* as shown in Figure 8.13.

Now I can see (Figure 8.13) that "Aimee" has requested to become my friend, and I can approve, deny, contact (Send Message), or mark Aimee as a spam sender. Unfortunately, Aimee isn't my type, and I don't know that she'd constitute the sort of initial

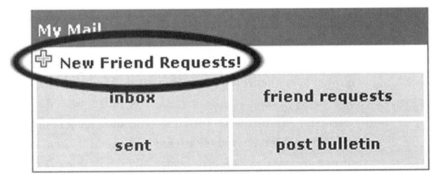

Figure 8.12 A new friend request flag is raised in your MySpace account Mail Box.

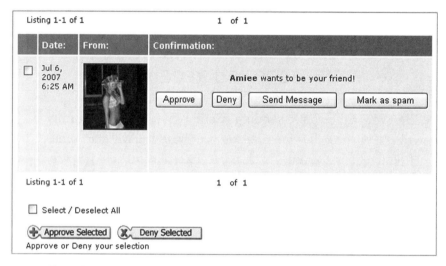

Figure 8.13 Review the member wanting to become your friend and decide whether or not you'll add this person as a friend.

clientele that I think would best represent my endeavors. Plus, I think Aimee is simply looking to pad her friends count and probably isn't really interested in what my page is all about. I'll deny her request and await others instead.

MySpace Tip

No, I'm not being a snob about Aimee's friend request, but I truthfully don't find much verity in her or her page's content (she refers to herself as a "Freeky Chick"). As much good as there is to be found on MySpace, there are a lot of not-so-good elements in the community. Be on the lookout for plenty of fake accounts as well as those promoting all manner of overactive promiscuity—you know what I mean.

Remember, it's *your* space and you needn't accept every friend request you receive, especially if you think it could taint the image you hope to project among the upstanding community members you strive to attract and entertain.

TO MAKE A FRIEND, BE A FRIEND

When two people entertain the idea of striking up a friendship, they sometimes ponder, "What's in it for me?" The same goes for the business scenario when one person considers opening a business based upon the clientele he or she can expect and the clientele must decide how useful or satisfying the products or services offered will be. For that reason, if you strive to make your MySpace page a compelling destination for your friends and one that effectively encourages them to sample your wares—online or at a physical place of business—then you need to give them plenty of reasons for spending time with you.

Therefore, be sure to make time to interact with your growing collection of friends, responding to their e-mail messages after they've joined your fold. Also, keep your page fresh by posting new videos, music links, and especially blog entries that will explain your latest interest, exploits, and offerings (see Chapter 9 for a full discussion of the mechanics of blogging at MySpace). And, as just referenced in the previous section of this chapter, be sure to keep your space populated with only the most sincere of friends, preventing any embarrassment or upset that others might experience if they navigate to one of your friends' pages and find the content to be less than admirable.

Establishing Your "Top Friends"

Although this might be misconstrued as a popularity contest of sorts (in some ways, it can be), you may have noticed a subtlety about the manner in which a user's page lists its friends. When you visit a MySpace page, you'll recall that, upon scrolling down the page a bit, the Friend Space contains the default profile images of friends a user has added. While folks who operate a personal page might want their best friends' photos (and links to *their* MySpace pages) to appear, those who operate a business of some sort often include some compelling friend selections in this area. That is, they recognize the drawing power of some friends—perhaps those associated with the same sort of business or those who might have complementary content—and they want visitors to recognize the company they keep.

Essentially, this works as a way for a particular user to establish a page that serves as a hub of sorts to more friends with more of the same good stuff he or she is delivering as well (and this works in reciprocal fashion when *your* page is of interest, and you're included in the most visible collection of friends in another users' Friend Space). That said, there's good reason to shuffle certain friends to the top of your friends list, and MySpace allows you to do this easily.

When you first begin establishing a friends list, MySpace will display the friends sequentially as you add them to your profile (remember how Tom became my first friend when I created my account, then Doombuggies showed up as friend number two). Additional friends' page links will be visibly added to the Friend Space on your page until you acquire more than four (a default setting within your account), and that's when you can begin to manage who gets front-page billing. By this, you'll be managing your "top friends," selecting not only how many top friends are visibly displayed on your MySpace page but also which ones will be displayed and in which order. To begin managing your top friends, click on the *Change My "Top Friends"* text link in the My Friend Space area of your profile page (see Figure 8.14).

When you click on the text link, you'll navigate to the Edit Your Top Friends screen as shown in Figure 8.15. Notice the pull-down selector where you can choose how many top friends to display on your page. Also, notice that the top friends you have selected can be reordered as you like by simply clicking and dragging them around one another on the Top Friends screen. When you've finished arranging your top friends, just click on the *Save Top Friends* button on the screen.

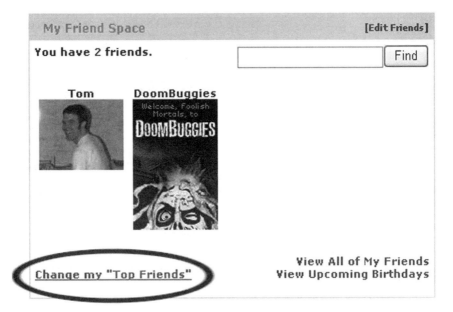

Figure 8.14 Click on the text link to begin managing your Top Friends list.

There is no "magic number" of friends you should display in your Friend Space, but you should try to keep it trim to avoid the area from upstaging the rest of your page's content. For this reason, it's recommended that you keep the number to about 25 displayed friends. Of course, if your business thrives when it behaves as a "who's who" destination and conspicuous name-dropping is needed to further your efforts (think of the classic Brown Derby restaurant in Hollywood and its well-known displays of entertainers' photos), then, by all means, increase the number of displayed friends.

MySpace Tip

If you're feeling bad for Aimee and others like her who may be fine enough folks but just not the sort of clientele you hope to attract to your page, you can still accept her friend

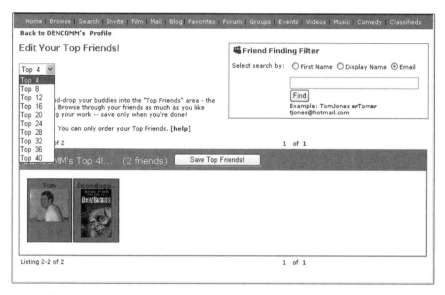

Figure 8.15 Modify the number of displayed friends images in your page's Friend Space, and rearrange them in a way that suits you.

request and simply relegate her out of your Top Friends space. Not everyone gets to be somebody's Top Friend (I'm not one of Doombuggies' top friends at this time), and that's fine enough. Just remember that your visitors can click to see all your friends when they visit your page, and if someone like Aimee is a bit too rowdy and rambunctious to keep along, even at the back of the room, well, you know what to do.

Keeping an Eye on Your Friends' Photos

One last point for the moment: Keep an eye on your Friend Space to see what images your accepted friends are posting. Remember that the friends you display at your page are simply links to their own pages, using the default photos they provide. Many folks update their default photos frequently, and it's up to you to ensure that one of your friends doesn't do something off color in a way that would offend you or your other friends.

If you established a good relationship with a friend who recently decided to display a donkey's backside or whatever, you might drop this friend a line to ask what's up. Otherwise, you can push the link farther back in your friends list or delete this person outright if he or she has suddenly turned for the worse. Don't be too prudish in your screening, but understand that you should strive to please the masses, especially when you have business objectives in mind and such an image change could undermine your efforts.

HOW MAKING FRIENDS CAN MAKE YOU MONEY

Now that you understand how to make and manage friends on MySpace, you should understand *why*. Beside the fact that you can strike up some interesting interactions and learn more about the folks who share MySpace with you, there is a practical purpose to all of this friend-making—leads, leverage, and lucrative entertaining. Those three Ls roll off the tongue nicely enough, but recognize what each means to you and your business.

- *Leads.* How many times have you heard, "It's not what you know, it's who you know?" Chances are that this is not an unfamiliar phrase to you, and, in business, the people you get to know are often the key to helping make your business a success. Some folks you get to know will know others who have the answers to some of the business questions you have or have solutions to some of the business challenges you are facing. After they get to know you and your goals, they sometimes offer up, "Oh, yeah, I know just the person who can help you with that; I'll pass along your name" (or, in the MySpace realm, it might go something like, "Yes, visit this person's MySpace page and add him to your friends list; he has what you're looking for").

Other folks you meet might be crucial to spreading the word about you and your page and are very gregarious in the way they feed information to a large segment of friends and acquaintances. These folks often know other key individuals who also have access to a large population of individuals who would be interested in your offerings (and you can read more about different persons and how they can help tip your business into success in Malcolm Gladwell's *The Tipping Point*).

- *Leverage.* Sometimes, the folks who become your friends bring a built-in audience to your page without much active effort on their part. These sorts of people can be good about adding you as a friend. Their page might be one of those "who's who" destinations where many folks visit and take note of the growing collection of friends' faces (or other such profile images) worthy of perusing directly. When you can become friended by such a person, you gain excellent exposure that amounts to a more passive yet prolific heralding of your page.

- *Lucrative entertaining.* And, to the point of this discussion, the more folks you can attract to your MySpace page, the more opportunity you have to share your place of business and your tempting offerings, be they online or off. After you've had the opportunity to service a sale or other such exchange with someone, you can expect this to encourage further word-of-mouth advertising for you. That, obviously, is the sort of friending you can take to the bank.

Of course, you'd never want to fully entrust the success of your page to a collection of friends, valued though they are, who just might have different points of view that might undermine your page's potential. Therefore, rather than let those friends do *all* the talking for you, you'll find that your best bet is to maintain a balance between what you friends do and say and what you want your visitors to unequivocally understand about you and your business. You'll need to step up to the virtual microphone yourself to speak your mind. Turn now to Chapter 9 to learn how easy it is to make your own voice heard within MySpace.

BLOGGING
WITH THE
BEST

Besides the friending activity that you'll manage on MySpace, blogging has proven to be the most interactive aspect of hosting a page and is key to keeping your friends, customers, and other visitors coming back on a regular basis. Although some would have you believe that the Internet is overrun and overdone with blogs, the fact is that blogs serve as a key draw for Netizens, and coupling a blog with a well-crafted MySpace page can give your business the *buzz* that you'd hope for.

MySpace Tip

If you already have a blog and you're actively keeping it updated, there's no need to shut it down in deference to the MySpace-hosted tool. Instead, simply include a link to your existing blog from within your MySpace layout. Naturally, the most obvious point of placement of such a link would be within the blog section of the MySpace page; add an active link to your blog so visitors can click and read just as easily as if you were hosting the blog directly within MySpace. And, don't forget to maintain an active link from your blog back to your MySpace page; some of your long-time blog visitors will surely be interested in viewing your MySpace page.

TOP TIPS FOR BEST-IN-CLASS BLOGS

Anyone who can type can post a blog, but that doesn't mean that anyone hosting a blog can successfully blog. While the attraction to blogs is their innate "personable" and "spontaneous" quality (bloggers write whatever's on their mind, and millions of Netizens love to read along), making a blog successful requires adhering to good writing and construction principles. Although you don't want to appear rigid or overly academic in your blogging (unless your blog will be about higher-level thinking and structured analysis), you can still be fresh and engaging while maintaining a sense of order and purpose in your prattling. That said, consider these tips for making your blog enticing yet tidy.

- *Be relevant.* When you visit a page that's all about collecting and appreciating antiques, you don't expect to read a blog that is devoted to political rants or even well-mannered expositions on the state of the political party system. Host a political page if this is your passion, but keep any blogs on an antique-related page relevant to antiquing or historical analysis of the provenance of particular items and the eras from which they came.

- *Make your point immediately.* Although your literature and composition professors might have drummed into your head that good writing has an opening paragraph that sets up the piece to come, online readers want to hear the conclusion first. Strange as it may seem, Net readers scan written pieces more than they would laboriously read them so their reading the first sentence or two from your blog, will determine whether they want to read more. Think of this as starting your blog entry with a *pull quote*, that essential line from a written piece that embodies the tone and thrust of the piece. Hook your readers with the point of your entry and then draw them in to read more about how you arrived at it.

- *Keep your writing trim.* Even though I have plenty of room in this book to faithfully expound on my topic points (and you'd expect nothing less from a book-length work), writing online is all about short bursts of information. Online readers are looking for a barrage of quick assertions with just enough fleshing out to support the ideas presented. When you approach your blogging, adopt a mindset of, "and another thing." This will put you in the make-a-point-quickly mode of thinking, and your readers will respond favorably.

- *Fire off bullets.* Again, with consideration to the online reader, understand that easily digestible *factoids* will be most satisfying. Therefore, use bulleted lists whenever possible (like this bulleted list you're reading now). Then craft each bullet point so that it can be stated in a sentence or two. With this approach, not only can you offer a visually clean and concise representation of the information you're sharing, but you can also do so with an economic approach to your text so that neither you nor your readers will need to wade through too much text.

- *Write with action.* Use convincing and even assertive language in your blogging. Rather than the weak attempt such as, "If you visit Coffee Spot, you might find that we have the best cup of coffee you've tasted," assert yourself with, "Come to Coffee Spot today—it has the best coffee around—guaranteed!" Readers like a blog that exudes confidence, and they often enjoy the challenge that a statement of conviction presents. They'll respond—you can count on it.

- *Write short sentences.* Remember, your blog is peppering your reader with fast facts and trim tidbits of information. Keep your sentences short, and they'll be more memorable to your readers.

- *Visually break up the structure.* Create frequent paragraphs (three or four sentences each, maximum). Again, use bulleted lists to incorporate further subdivision of the information. The paragraph breaks and indented bulleted lists introduce just enough whitespace to make your blog easy on the eyes and easy for readers to extract key information.

- *Embed links.* Many times there's more to say than might be appropriate in your blog. If that's the case, lead your readers to a place where you can say it—and they can choose to read it. Your blog will often serve as a "hook" or a "tickler" to capture your readers' attention; provide a link to the full story if they're interested in reading more. If not, they can move along to the rest of your concise blog entry without bailing out prematurely.

- *Check your spelling.* You knew this was coming, and so here it is: Spelling still counts. For that matter, so does proper punctuation and good grammar. The basics of sound writing apply, even in the on-the-go world of the Internet. Make sure your blog is well crafted in this regard lest you undermine your credibility with the first *mispelt* word. See what I mean?

WHAT SHOULD YOU BLOG ABOUT?

When it comes to deciding what to talk about in your blog, you're pretty much on your own—it is *your* blog. But, wait. There are a few tips I can share to help you get past the "blank page" syndrome. Although the most interesting blogs seem to consist of spontaneous outpourings of tip-of-the-tongue trivia and whatnot, the best ones are actually well-planned dissertations *written* to read as if they're the morning's waking ramblings. Blogs come in many forms and use tones and styles appropriate to the material and the audience that will read them. So as you ponder what it is that you'll blog about, think back to the initial planning of your MySpace page (from the discussion in Chapter 2) and recall the reasons you decided to join this community in the first place. With that in mind and as you recall the audience you sought to attract with your page, write about the topics your targeted visitors will actively seek out.

BUILDING A BLOG AT MySPACE

If your MySpace experience will also be your introduction to blogging, that's great because MySpace has the tools to help you get started. Don't get caught up in any of the naysayer's rants that there are "cooler" blog spaces out there; the point of a blog is to write and share thoughts, ideas, and insight that others will want to read. — Who cares what tool you use, right? And since your MySpace page is truly taking shape and you're building a community of friends and repeat visitors, it's time to get blogging.

Creating Your Blog Space at MySpace

To get started, log in to your MySpace account, and, from your account maintenance home page, locate and click on the text link, *Manage Blog* (see Figure 9.1).

Upon clicking on the *Manage Blog* link, you'll navigate to the Blog Control Center screen as shown in Figure 9.2. This is the screen where you can create new blogs, view existing blogs (including an archive of past blogs you've posted), check statistics of your

Figure 9.1 Begin creating your blog from the account maintenance main screen.

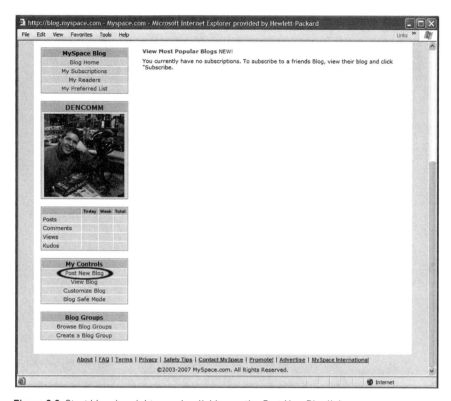

Figure 9.2 Start blogging right away by clicking on the *Post New Blog* link.

blog readership, and even customize your blog content and appearance. If you've never written a blog (or haven't written much at all), don't fear; it's *your* blog, and it's your space to post your thoughts, ideas, and business activity. To get started on your first blog entry, just click on the *Post New Blog* text link, circled in Figure 9.2.

When you're creating a new blog posting, you'll work in the Post a new Blog Entry screen as shown in Figure 9.3. Here's a rundown of the elements you'll manage while you create your entry:

- *Subject.* Make this a compelling title for your blog entry since it's all that will be displayed in the blog area on your front page.

- *Category.* You can select from a drop-down menu of category selections if you want your blog to be category-specific

Figure 9.3 There are plenty of tools and options you can use on the Post a new Blog Entry screen.

or you just need a bit of help deciding what you want to blog about (but since we're talking about your business here, that shouldn't be a problem).

- *Body.* Here's where you start writing. Recall the blog tips mentioned previously in this chapter and then have at it. Notice that you can alter the font, color, and size of the text in your post. Also, there are additional buttons where you

can include URL links to other Web pages (perhaps an article or image you want to reference but not include directly
within the body of your post), embed images directly
within your post, keyboard symbols for special typewritten
characters, and even *emoticons*. Finally, you can select a
background color if you want your post to be visually set off
on your page.

- *Tell us . . . .* This is a fun selector that allows you to include
  an image of a CD, a book, a DVD, or video game if you
  want to let folks know what's entertaining you at the
  moment. Use this to tie in the blog to the overall theme of
  your page, or don't use it if it wouldn't really pertain to your
  blog posting.

- *Current mood.* Again, this serves as a barometer of your
  present feeling and is fun to use if you're hosting a personal page but probably doesn't apply to a business-
  oriented layout. Still, it's your choice to select from the
  drop-down menu of moods if you like.

- *Comments.* This is where the interactivity of MySpace
  comes into play. You can allow visitors who read your blog
  to post their comments to a particular entry, opening up
  potential for a healthy back-and-forth dialogue. This is
  great if you'll be discussing matters of the day, of your business direction, what-should-we-do-next opinion polls, and
  so on. If you check this box, you'll disable visitors from
  being able to post comments and "kudos" to your posting.
  Feel free to enable and disable different blog postings as
  suits your needs.

- *Privacy.* Here's where you can control who sees your blog,
  from everybody (select Public) to nobody but you (select
  Diary). Additionally, you can limit viewership to only your
  friends (select Friends) or only selected individuals from
  your friends list (select Preferred List).

MySpace Tip

Posting certain blogs for Preferred List viewing is a great way to maintain an active flow of information to friends with whom you might partner in your endeavors. If you own a coffeehouse and you need to maintain information flow to musicians who will perform at your venue, restrict that information just to those folks. If you're manufacturing new products and wish to maintain a status log of your progress, make it readable only to those folks with whom you're working. You get the idea.

- *Podcast enclosure.* If you actively maintain a podcast—one of your own or a favorite published by someone else—enter the URL link here to include it in your blog posting. This is a great way to provide a bit of commentary on a topic that is raised in the podcast and then provide the actual cast for your readers to listen to themselves.

After you've written the body content and selected the various settings, simply click on the *Preview & Post* button (Figure 9.3) to see the result of your work (as shown in Figure 9.4).

If you like what you see, click on the *Post Blog* button, and you'll find that a new blog entry is available on your MySpace homepage (see Figure 9.5).

Assuming you made your blog post public, visitors will see the subject of your post and can click on the *View more* text link to read the entire blog post (see Figure 9.6). And, just like that, you're blogging.

CUSTOMIZING YOUR BLOG

As you can tell, MySpace is all about customization, giving you almost complete control of what you include on your page and how you choose to display it; blogs are no different. If the simple look

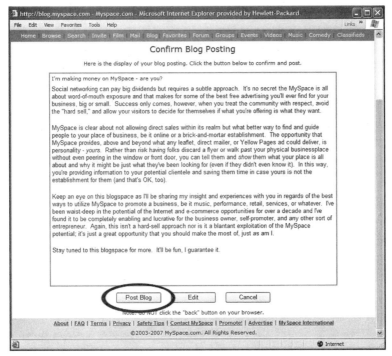

Figure 9.4 Review the content of your blog post before you release it to your MySpace page.

Figure 9.5 As easy as that, your blog post is now on your MySpace page.

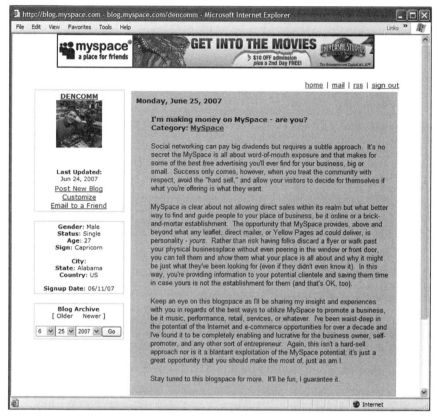

Figure 9.6 For those to whom you've granted access to your blog, here's a simple example of what they can expect to see when they decide to click on *View more.*

of a blog isn't enough for you (although you should still take care not to overdo a good thing), then click on the *Customize Blog* text link from the Blog Control Screen (refer back to Figure 9-2). When you click on the link, you'll navigate to the Customize My Blog screen, as shown in Figure 9.7.

Here you can customize the way your blog display screens look beyond the simple design shown in Figure 9.6. The customization is very similar to the profile customization you did in Chapter 6—you can change background colors, border colors, font colors, font types, and more. I've done some simple tweaks by enabling a custom header for my blog page that ties in the Dencomm logo design as well as the color schemes that are complementary to my home page layout. I clicked on the *Preview* text

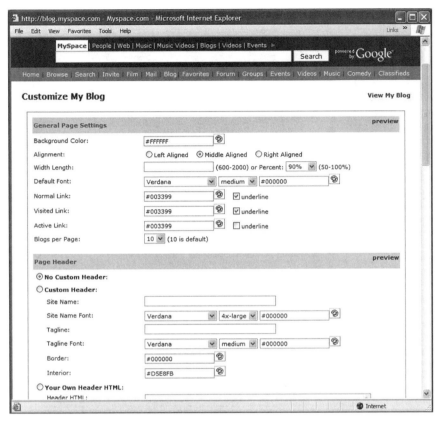

Figure 9.7 More customizing opportunities await you on your MySpace blog page with this Customize My Blog screen.

links to check my progress, and, when I was satisfied, I clicked on the *Update* button located at the bottom of the customization screen. With just a few click-and-choose selections, I quickly customized my blog page to look like what you see in Figure 9.8.

MySpace Tip

Incidentally, you can use CSS code on your blog page if you like. Within the customization options is an area where you can paste in CSS code to truly take control of your blog page (refer back to Chapter 6).

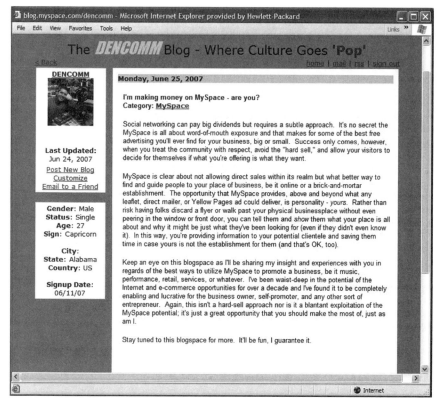

Figure 9.8 It's not too fancy, but it brings in some continuity of design; these simple customizations relate back to my home page layout.

Before leaving the topic of blog page customizations, understand that the slinging of HTML and CSS code can sometimes make a mess of things in cases where the code is not quite right. Often a simple misplaced or omitted tag can render a customization job unreadable. If ever you find that your customized page is a garbled mess, return to the Blog Control Center and select the *Blog Safe Mode* text link (refer to Figure 9.2) where you can see your blog page in all its HTML and CSS glory. From this view, you can review all tags to see where the problem might lie (see Figure 9.9).

And if you simply want to put everything back to the plain-Jane format that MySpace offered at the outset, click on the *Restore to Default* button at the bottom of the Customize Blog screen. Just

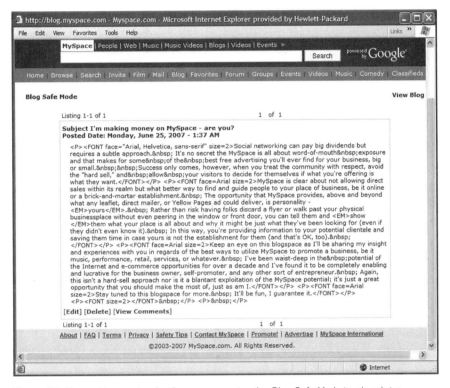

Figure 9.9 If your blog customizations go awry, try the *Blog Safe Mode* to pinpoint a wayward HTML or CSS tag.

remember, the key to a compelling blog isn't so much the dressing as it is the content—so get blogging. And after you've done that, take a look at Chapter 10 to harness a few other key communication tools that will help you gain the greatest traction for your MySpace page and purpose.

MAKING THE MOST OF COMMENTS, MESSAGES, AND BULLETINS

By now, you've come to understand the key elements to becoming a visible and contributing member of the MySpace community. You understand how to create your profile, how to keep it under wraps while you add content and other adornments to your profile, and how to blow the trumpet to let others know you have arrived. Now it's time to begin interacting in earnest. Although you're free to modify the content of your page whenever you like (and you're encouraged to do so to keep your page fresh and inviting), you should spend time marketing yourself and your business via your MySpace presence. Again, you aren't allowed to sell directly from within MySpace, but you're free to spread the word about your interests, your endeavors, and the things you have to offer to others.

In this final chapter in this part of the book, you'll discover how easy it is to make announcements about your business—in a one-on-one fashion, in a group distribution method, or simply by tacking up a virtual banner to let any and all visitors know what's up in your neck of the MySpace woods. This is where you can harness the ease-of-reach potential that MySpace offers and where you can truly springboard the buzz about *your space*.

TO MAKE A FRIEND, BE A FRIEND

When two people entertain the idea of striking up a friendship, they sometimes ponder, "What's in it for me?" This is more often the case for the business scenario when one person considers opening a business based upon the clientele she can expect and the patron weighs how useful or satisfying the products or services offered will be. For that reason, if you strive to make your MySpace page a compelling destination for your friends and one that effectively encourages them to sample your wares, online or at a physical place of business, then you need to give them plenty of reasons why they should spend time with you.

Therefore, be sure to make time to interact with your growing collection of friends, responding to their e-mail messages after they've joined your fold. Also, keep your page fresh by posting new videos, music links, and especially blog entries that will explain your latest interest, exploits, and offerings (see Chapter 9 for a full discussion of the mechanics of blogging at MySpace). And, as referenced in the discussion of Chapter 8, be sure to keep your space populated with only the most sincere of friends, preventing any embarrassment or upset that others might experience if they navigate to one of your friend's pages and find the content to be less than admirable.

CONNECTING WITH YOUR FRIENDS

As your friends list continues to grow (and, rest assured, it will), you might want to begin utilizing your friends' contact information in a way that makes it easier for you to interact with them and share interesting facts, developments, and offers. At MySpace, there are several ways to interact with your friends, and you have the freedom to utilize one, some, or all of the communication methods that will help you continue to reach out and stay in touch.

Using Comments to Get the Ball Rolling

The easiest way to engage your friends in a nonintrusive manner is to leave comments on their pages when they add you as a friend. Within the MySpace community, it can be considered bad form *not* to post a "thanks for the add" acknowledgment when you're added to another's friend list. Leaving a comment is as easy as visiting the new friend's page and clicking on the *Add Comment* text link located atop the Friends Comments area of the page. Enter the comment in the appropriately labeled text box and click on the *Post a Comment* button (see Figure 10.1).

Next, MySpace will provide an authorization screen that requests that you type in the graphically presented letters or numbers (case insensitive) and then click on the *Post a Comment* button again (see Figure 10.2).

When you do, you'll see a comment confirmation note. The result of this simple activity is that your comment, accompanied by your own default image, will now be visible to all on your new friend's page (see Figure 10.3).

Figure 10.1 Show your thanks to your new friend by adding a comment to his or her page.

Figure 10.2 Enter the authorization code as shown and click on *Post a Comment* button once more.

Sending Messages

The simplest way to communicate with your MySpace friends directly is to send a traditional electronic message. Just as you would manage any other e-mail communication, you can access your MySpace profile page and use the messaging functionality to send mail to your friends. From any MySpace page you visit, locate the *Send Message* text link, click on it, and create a message to

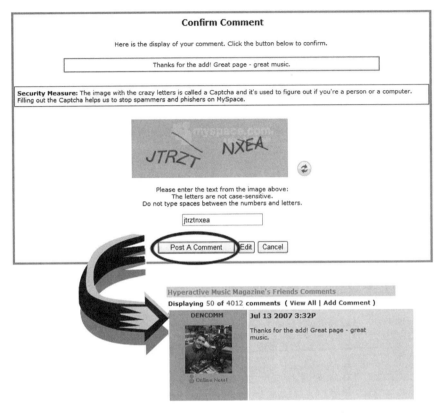

Figure 10.3 After a simple confirmation, your comment has been added to your new friend's page.

send (see Figure 10.4). When you click on the *Send* button, your message will be routed to the page owner's inbox. When you begin friending with others, they'll likely send messages to you as well.

Using the Address Book to Manage Your Friends

As your friends list begins to grow, you might find use in keeping track of their contact information by adding them to your own address book. From here, you can also create segmented lists to categorize your friends such as "Poker Gang," "Pop Culture Quiz Contestants," and so on. Begin by creating contacts in your address nook by looking to the My Mail area on your MySpace account

Figure 10.4 Sending individual messages at MySpace is easy.

page and then click on the *Address Book* text link in your Mail Center Inbox (see Figure 10.5).

Next, create contacts within your address book, those you'll be able to utilize one by one or collect into a distribution list of many names. Click on the *Add a Contact* text link and enter the information about the contact on the contact screen. Once that's done, click on the *Lists* text link, type in a list name in the appropriate box, and click on the *Add* button. When you do, the screen will refresh to provide you with a selection box of all of your current contacts from which you can select to add to the new contact list you're creating. These steps are shown in Figure 10.6.

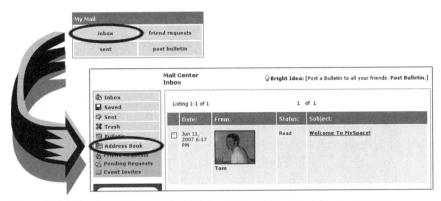

Figure 10.5 To begin creating a contact list, locate the address book for your account.

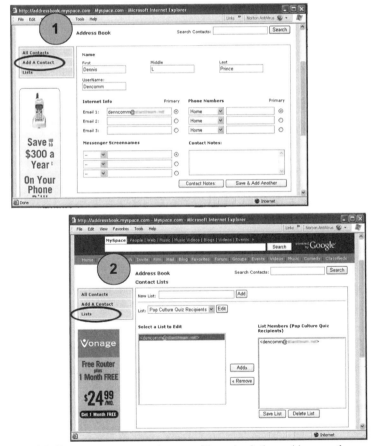

Figure 10.6 First create a contact in your address book then add names from your contacts to the Contact List.

Bulk Communication Made Easy with Bulletins

Sending messages one by one might be too cumbersome for your needs, especially if you want to let many friends know about something, perhaps about the products or services you offer that might be of interest to them. The answer to getting more coverage with less effort comes in the way of bulletins.

Bulletins and flyers have long been a staple of direct marketing, serving as the method for getting the word out about great new products or exciting upcoming events. At MySpace, you can save yourself the foot time yet achieve the same result when you post a bulletin to your friends. In fact, I regularly receive bulletins from my friends; an example is shown in Figure 10.7.

If you want to create a bulletin of your own, simply click on the *post bulletin* text link within the My Mail area of your profile page and then enter the bulletin name and text, click on the *Post* button, and your bulletin is on its way to all your current friends. See Figure 10.8. When it comes to efficiency in communicating with your clientele, bulletins are the way to go.

WAIT! YOU *CAN* SELL AT MySPACE?

There is a mechanism available for limited merchandising at MySpace—classified ads. Looking like an easy knockoff of craigslist, MySpace provides an area where community members can post classified ads, just like those you find elsewhere online or in your local newspaper. Don't expect that you can make a fortune utilizing the MySpace classifieds, but you can find some interesting "market demographics" information when you scan what others are offering or actively looking for. To peruse the ads yourself, just click on the *Classifieds* text link on the MySpace main toolbar and, upon doing so, you'll navigate to the Classifieds main screen (see Figure 10.9)

Figure 10.7 My friend, MojoRisin, posted this bulletin to me and the rest of his friends letting us know of the upcoming live entertainment at the Mojo Risin' Coffee House.

On the Classifieds main screen, you'll notice that you can search ads in a couple of different ways:

1. By city, changeable as noted in callout 1 in Figure 10.9.

2. By key word and category as noted in callout 2 in Figure 10.9.

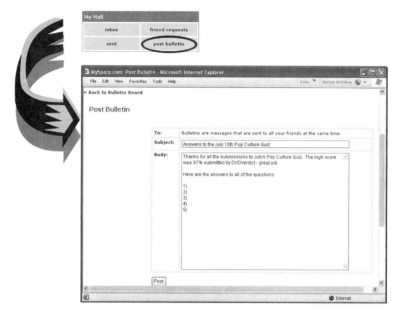

Figure 10.8 Post your own bulletin with a few clicks on MySpace.

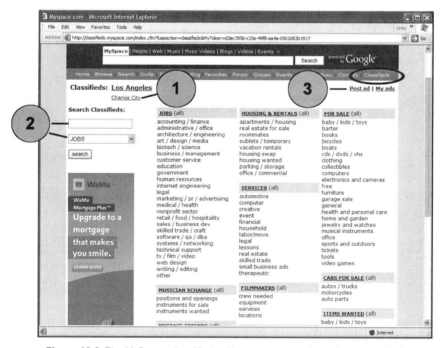

Figure 10.9 The MySpace classifieds allow you to see what others are offering and looking for, information that is useful in helping you better understand the community's consumption habits.

MySpace Tip

You might notice that the city designation of the MySpace classifieds defaults to your own profile's designated city.

If you want to play around with the classified ads, consider posting an item for sale, a service you offer, or a product or service you're looking for (and this can be another avenue for finding help with your business such as Web design and such). To post an ad of your own, simply click on the *Post ad* text link, noted in callout 3 in Figure 10.9. When you do, you'll arrive at a simple ad creation page as shown in Figure 10.10.

On the classified ad posting screen, you'll notice that the selected posting city is provided (you can change it by clicking on the *Change City* text link). All you need do is:

1. Select an ad type category and subcategory by using the pull-down selectors.

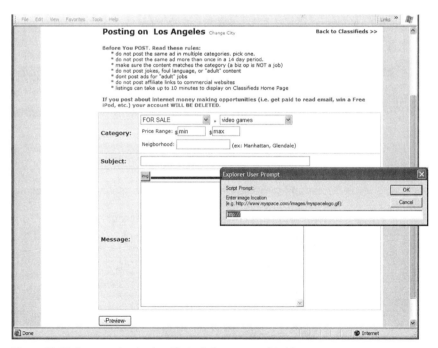

Figure 10.10 Create a simple classified ad of your own with this easy-to-use screen.

2. Specify a price range for your listing.

3. Specify a local neighborhood (if you like, though this is not required, and you may wish to leave this blank to maintain privacy).

4. Type in a subject line for your ad (limited to 60 characters including spaces).

5. Include an image by clicking on the *IMG* button and entering the URL location of the picture you wish to attach (similar to the way you selected a hosted default image for your MySpace profile).

6. Type in a description for the ad in the Message box.

7. Preview the ad by clicking on the *Preview* button.

You can preview your ad and edit it if you want to make additional changes. When you're satisfied with it, click on the *Post Ad* button on the preview screen, and you're done.

MySpace Tip

Be sure to keep in mind the rules for posting ads on MySpace; they're clearly noted on the ad creation screen (refer to Figure 10.10) but are definitely worth repeating verbatim here:

- do not post the same ad in multiple categories. pick one.

- do not post the same ad more than once in a 14 day period.

- make sure the content matches the category (a biz op is NOT a job)

- do not post jokes, foul language, or "adult" content

- do not post ads for "adult" jobs

- do not post affiliate links to commercial Web sites

If you break any of these rules, your ad is subject to deletion and, in some cases, your MySpace account can also be deleted.

Again, using MySpace classifieds isn't a viable method to manage your business endeavors, but it can help you understand some of the wants and needs of people in particular locales. Use that information to determine if you need to make any adjustments to your marketing approach and the content on your page to better connect with your target audience.

WHAT ABOUT THE OTHER FEATURES OF MySPACE?

Certainly, I haven't shown you *absolutely everything* that MySpace has to offer, and that's by design. Rather than go on and on about all the other tools available to you within MySpace—the calendar, events, groups, instant messaging, the forum, and others—I've settled on the key functions that you can use quickly and easily to benefit your business.

Now that you've come this far, though, you should be familiar enough with the overall landscape to be able to return to explore some of these other avenues available to you to further enlarge your MySpace presence. Just remember, too much of a good thing isn't a good thing. Keep focused on your business objectives, understand the needs and likes of your target audience, and present the right amount of form and function that will satisfy the people you're trying to reach and help you improve your business results.

With that said, turn now to Part 3 to review some other pages and to see how other Spacers have done just as I've said—used the right amount of MySpace features—to present compelling presentations that serve their goals well.

LOOK AND LEARN—**CASE STUDIES** OF SUCCESSFUL **MySPACE** MARKETERS

CASE STUDY:
LACKLUSTER FILMS' *A.*
(ANONYMOUS)

This section of the book is a look at the ways some people have harnessed MySpace to further their businesses or business-minded interests. It begins with a visit to the local art-house cinema for a peek at Lackluster Pictures' A. *(anonymous)* promotional page, www.myspace.com/anonymousmovie.

WHAT IS *A. (ANONYMOUS)*?

Long ago, budding filmmakers without recognition or significant funding were relegated to making their amateur films on 8-mm or 16-mm stock. They hoped that they might find some obscure venue to screen their work for anybody who might unknowingly wander in to take a look. That's all changed now with the advent of the digital video camera and computer-based film editing and post-production processing. Now, aspiring directors and producers can deliver rather impressive results on a shoestring budget, and, thanks to the Internet and MySpace, screenings can take place anytime and anywhere and be viewable by anyone. Director Daniel Bowers wisely secured a MySpace URL where he could host his own promotional page to herald the coming of his newest feature, *A. (anonymous)*.

SIZING UP LACKLUSTER PICTURES' *A. (ANONYMOUS)* PAGE

There's a vibrant feel to the *A. (anonymous)* page; the solid golden-rod-colored background works to give perfect contrast to the film's poster design as well as the promotional photos and film scenes. Moreover, this page does well with the following additional aspects (called out in Figure 11.1):

1. Appropriately, the page's default image is that of the film's poster, ensuring that anywhere *A. (anonymous)* shows up as a friend, it will be deftly promoting itself.

2. Director Bowers includes a screening room of sorts where visitors can view the official trailer for *A. (anonymous)* as well as excerpts his other works.

Figure 11.1 The *A. (anonymous)* page at MySpace.com.

3. Large images of scenes from the film and of the actors are included to further convey the gist of the plot.

4. And Bowers also has updated this page to include an active link that allows visitors to navigate to Amazon.com to actually purchase a DVD of the movie.

In the final analysis, the *A. (anonymous)* page at MySpace does an admirable job of promoting the film with a clean and generally uncluttered design. It's easy to learn about the film and the actors from the images and slideshow included on the page. The director's film clips and trailer for the feature film help visitors learn more about what they can expect from screening it for themselves. And, the direct link to purchase the DVD makes this a perfect use of a page designed to announce and distribute the picture in a way that filmmakers from 20 years ago never could have envisioned.

CASE STUDY:
HYPERACTIVE MUSIC MAGAZINE

I f you like your music raw and with a frequent splash of South-west sensibility, look no further than *Hyperactive Music Magazine* at www.myspace.com/ hyperactivemusic-magazine. This is a companion site to the magazine's official Web presence, www.hyperactivemusicmag. com, which is also a companion to the newsstand version of the magazine itself. The *Hyperactive* team is rounding the various multimedia bases.

WHAT IS THE *HYPERACTIVE MUSIC MAGAZINE*?

There's a pleasingly gritty feel to *Hyperactive,* possibly the by-product of its Albuquerque, New Mexico, location but more likely thanks to its grassroots approach to insightful commentary on the indie music scene. Publisher and owner Ally Shaw has reached out to cover all genres of music but has decidedly bent this internationally distributed magazine toward unsigned and up-and-coming talent. This makes a *Hyperactive* presence on MySpace an easy fit since it's definitely a self-made, self-promoted endeavor that has been successful in spawning nine bimonthly issues with no signs of stopping.

And Shaw has smartly created a companion MySpace page, www.myspace.com/hyperactivefestival, which promotes the magazine's sponsored *Hyperactive* Music Festival and Conference in Albuquerque, an event that assembles 200 bands plus music industry executives and fans.

SIZING UP THE *HYPERACTIVE MUSIC MAGAZINE* PAGE

The *Hyperactive Music Magazine* page at MySpace might look sparse on first glance, but it's clear about its purpose—to feature music. The clean design looks almost unfinished and a bit raw (which I find suitable to its indie nature), but it immediately features a jukebox that offers a selection of tunes from currently featured bands. Additionally, the page offers these attractions (called out in Figure 12.1):

1. As mentioned, *Hyperactive* is all about the music, and a featured song begins streaming from the jukebox as soon as the page loads.

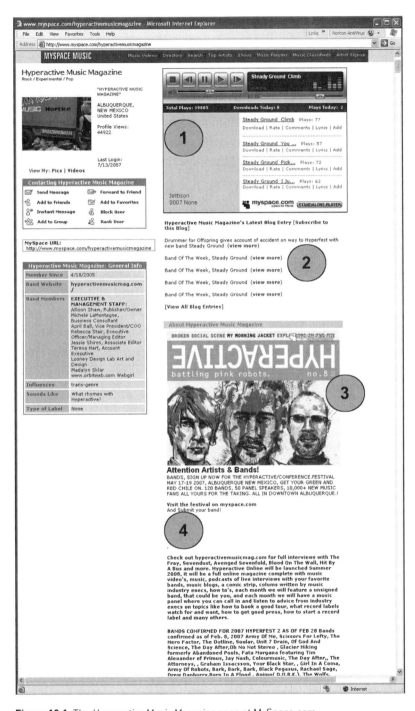

Figure 12.1 The *Hyperactive Music Magazine* page at MySpace.com

2. The blog area features well-written blurbs about the featured bands.

3. The slideshow delivers images of bands, the *Hyperactive* staff, and images of *Hyperactive Music Magazine* covers.

4. And, the page offers generous information about *Hyperactive*, the bands it has been covering, and news of the upcoming *Hyperactive* Music Festival and Conference.

The bottom line is that the *Hyperactive Music Magazine* page at MySpace isn't the most dazzling design on the block, and that clearly works in its favor. It wisely focuses on the music while still providing images and information about the printed publication, the sponsored festival, and the bands. Ultimately, this translates into increased awareness of the bands featured and helps boost participation and attendance at the festivals. These folks have dispensed with laborious handbill and phone-bank marketing tactics, reaching more eyes and ears while eliminating the otherwise burdensome PR costs.

CASE STUDY:
MOJO RISIN'
COFFEE HOUSE

For a great cup of java paired with a steady flow of energizing music from upcoming talent, make your way to Mojo Risin' Coffee House at www.myspace.com/mojorisincoffee.

WHAT IS THE MOJO RISIN' COFFEE HOUSE?

Without a doubt, owner Jack Mullen has determined that his target audience is the sort that likes its music live, its beverages smooth, and the overall experience natural. Since opening its doors in 2005, the Mojo Risin' Coffee House, located in Houston, Texas, has provided a stage and microphone to the area's burgeoning population of local musicians. The cozy stage is flanked by colorfully hand-painted tables and chairs that harken back to the days of turning on, tuning in, and dropping out (these days, though, the chemical of choice is caffeine since you won't find alcohol or any other mood enhancers within its walls). Besides attracting a steady flow of Houstonians to sample the offerings—consumable and musical—Mojo Risin' Coffee House is also hosting numerous journalists eager to find out what makes this grind so enticing.

SIZING UP THE MOJO RISIN' COFFEE PAGE

The Mojo Risin' Coffee House page at MySpace has incredible ambience that is reminiscent of the Haight-Ashbury experience yet has plenty of current-day technology to let you know that this is no outdated affair. The page offers the address of the Houston, Texas destination, a contact e-mail address, and the added attraction that it's a Wi-Fi enabled Internet hot spot. Additionally, the page includes these key elements (noted in Figure 13.1):

1. The page immediately conveys a feel of the modern music scene (wisely, the profile was established as a music page) but is also infused with an appealing vintage flavor of a kick-back coffee house thanks to the 1960s era background and quasi-psychedelic Mojo Risin' logo (that looks pleasingly like a classic K-Tel record cover).

2. It immediately provides a list of upcoming live performances utilizing the calendar function to post the list of musical events, enticing fans to come to the café to watch their favorite bands and hopefully buy a few drinks while they are there.

3. It offers a slideshow of images showing the interior of the coffeehouse with emphasis on the performers that have

Figure 13.1 The Mojo Risin' Coffee House page at MySpace.com.

graced its stage (this is a great way to build a buzz about the site, using the old "you promote me and I'll promote you" handshake with the featured talent).

4. And the page proudly displays the other attractions of the coffeehouse—the food, beverages, and tempting dessert table.

The page design serves as the perfect "handbill" to help the uninitiated discover what Mojo Risin' Coffee House is all about. It's vibrant but laid back, tech-savvy but temporal, and definitely makes a compelling invitation to visit the establishment at the earliest opportunity. You won't find an alternate Web site for Mojo Risin' Coffee House at this time, but, with a MySpace page design this good, there's really no need.

CASE STUDY:
DVD VERDICT

I f film and television is your passion, be certain to pay a visit to the DVD Verdict page at www.myspace.com/dvdverdict.

WHAT IS DVD VERDICT?

Michael Stailey serves as the chief editor and presiding "chief justice" of DVD Verdict (www.dvdverdict.com). The site was established in 1998, riding the cutting edge of the emerging DVD technology, assuming the task of reporting on the state of the emerging medium and helping the consuming public determine if a shiny new disc was worthy of a purchase or rental. Adopting a decidedly irreverent tone that would become its trademark attraction, the DVD Verdict conclave of "judges" would dutifully review the facts of each case, weigh the evidentiary submissions, and ultimately determine if a DVD would be deemed innocent or guilty. The film reviews are top-notch, and the staff of over 40 film critics (those are the judges) analyze each and every disc with admirable yet entertaining legalistic diligence.

The DVD Verdict page at MySpace was launched during the summer of 2006 and has proven to be a significantly worthwhile endeavor for Stailey and his staff. Although a logical source of traffic would come to the DVD Verdict Web site by way of the widely used Internet Movie Database (www.imdb.com), Stailey has indicated that this MySpace page has usurped IMDb as the main avenue for newcomers, this page now being the top referring site.

SIZING UP THE DVD VERDICT PAGE

The DVD Verdict page at MySpace is dutifully constructed and easy to digest, just like a legal brief should be. The page features these key elements (called out in Figure 14.1) that solidly support the DVD Verdict mission:

1. It utilizes the DVD Verdict logo as its default profile image to immediately establish its brand.

2. It wastes no time in providing visitors with immediate links to what they would expect—DVD reviews.

3. It also offers an array of links that will navigate visitors to key areas of the DVD Verdict Web site, thereby providing another avenue for exploring all the main site has to offer.

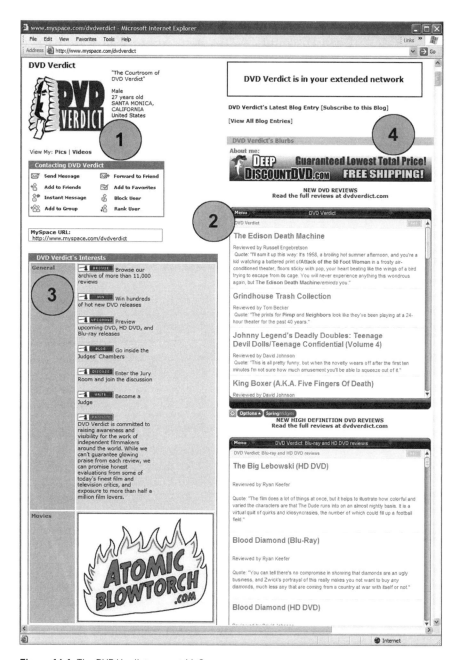

Figure 14.1 The DVD Verdict page at MySpace.com.

4. In order to actually collect revenue to further its mission, it smartly provides a link to an affiliate consumer site (Deep Discount DVD) where commissions are earned whenever visitors navigate the link and purchase DVDs or other products.

Overall, the page design is sleek and easy to navigate. It loads quickly and delivers the goods fast. The DVD Verdict page at MySpace is useful, usable, and adeptly captures the eyes of the community. When it comes making good use of the MySpace potential, the DVD Verdict page is certainly innocent of any transgressions.

CASE STUDY:
SEW DARN
CUTE

J ust as its name promises, this is a simple page that is darn cute. It's not presumptuous, nor is it pompous in its approach. It's just a page devoted to the craft-minded population that is seeking the comfort and coziness of hobbies, all found at www.myspace.com/sewdarncute.

WHAT IS SEW DARN CUTE?

Drop the knitting needles and hold onto that hot glue gun because Jenny Ryan has burst onto the felt-and-fabric scene with her Sew Darn Cute page, Web site, and biannual do-it-yourself extravaganza, Felt Club XL. Based in Los Angeles, California, Ms. Ryan has brought hand-fashioned creations forward into the New Millennium with an emphasis on color and a dash of creative kookiness. Whether she's showing how to fabricate your own cutesy crafts or offering her own creations for sale, Ryan appears to be the Martha Stewart of MySpace. Her energy and passion for this pastime is evident in her blog entries as well as within the copy found on her direct-sales Web site, www.sewdarncute.com. She's in it for the fun but is also making a financial gain along the way. From where I'm sitting, it seems to make a great combination that's also attracted nearly a thousand MySpace friends.

SIZING UP THE SEW DARN CUTE PAGE

It has the immediate familiar feel of Fisher-Price paired with 1950s kitsch. The page design is simple and even soothing to view. Most poignantly, this page sews up success thanks to these little details (called out in Figure 15.1):

1. Call me a sucker for a pretty face, but this classic little cutie that adorns the Sew Darn Cute default image is just fun to behold. As it appears here and would appear on a friend link, this little darling of yesterday is sure to encourage a curious click.

2. The blog entries here are plentiful and timely, covering all aspects of interest, from sales-oriented specials (free shipping

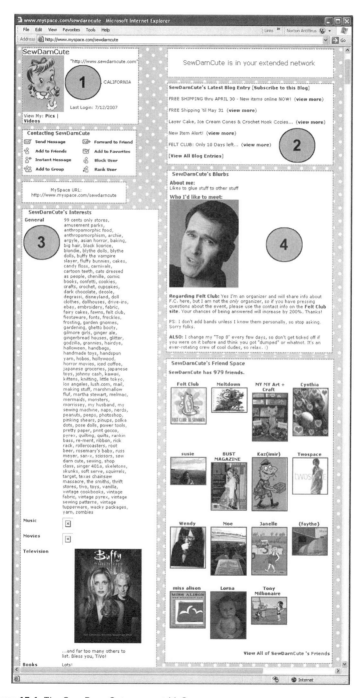

Figure 15.1 The Sew Darn Cute page at MySpace.com.

on purchases) to how-to dissertations on crafty creations, there's always something fun to read here.

3. While it might seem more personal than business in its orientation, the voluminous amount of stated *Interests* here work perfectly into the fabric of crafters—theirs *is* a world based upon friendships and sharing common interests. By offering such a hefty amount of interest topics here, the Sew Darn Cute page reaches out to other like-minded folks to help strike up friendships enjoyed while crafting something creative.

4. Although it's amusing that Ms. Ryan has something of a crush on half-man, mostly chin actor Bruce Campbell, the interest in the blurb space here is how friends are notified that they will be randomly and frequently rotated out of the Top Friends spot. Ms. Ryan demonstrates that this is a hobby to enjoy with friends—all of them—and helps foster a mood of sharing her time equally among her crafting friends.

Sew Darn Cute has a properly pitched design that is as inviting as it is inspiring (with crafters always hungry to read about their peers' great ideas and tips). Ms. Ryan knows her audience well and provides a MySpace page that is dolled up just right and positions her ideas alongside revenue-generating supplies and craft-event promotions, all without succumbing to becoming a rhinestone-encrusted aberration.

CASE STUDY:
RETRO ATTIC

I f you're wondering what happened to the sleek and impeccably shifting fashions of the 1950s and 1960s, all you need do is climb up the stairs to the Retro Attic at www.myspace.com/retroattic. At first, you won't believe these are the fashions of yesteryear, yet, very quickly, you'll become mesmerized by the fusion of art and accessorizing in a way that is woefully extinct today.

WHAT IS RETRO ATTIC?

As the founder confesses, her love of all things retro began in her childhood when she was pulled along by her parents to dip into one antique shop after another. One restroom visit for this weary waif introduced her to a cubby decorated in covers from *Vogue* and *Harper's Bazaar* and infused her with what would become a life-long passion for the style and mystique of a bygone era. An active seller at eBay and eCrater, Retro Attic is never at a loss for inventory to satisfy those with similar refined tastes. And it keeps the information and conversation flowing about the latest trends and offerings it has available for sale. Just as enticing is the wealth of blog content the Retro Attic offers up, at MySpace as well as several other sites within the blogosphere. When it comes to vintage fashion and accessories, Retro Attic is rarely at a loss for words.

SIZING UP THE RETRO ATTIC PAGE

You can practically hear the sweet and sentimental strains of Henry Mancini the moment you visit the Retro Attic page at MySpace (although there is no audio content on the page; an opportunity that should be addressed, in my opinion). No matter, though, because this page has some well-designed elements that make excellent use of the MySpace experience (called out in Figure 16.1):

1. The vertically extended default image says it all, visually, with its slender design subtly conveying the same sort of long-legged elegance that inspired Retro Attic in the first place—vintage fashion design a la *Vogue* and *Harper's Bazaar* magazines. Here, it matches the over-slender page design beautifully.

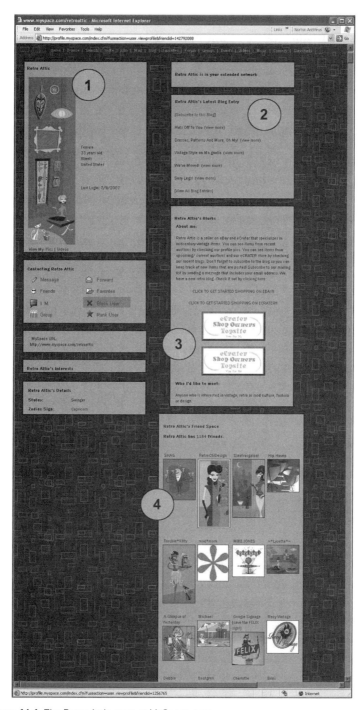

Figure 16.1 The Retro Attic page at MySpace.com.

2. There is great blogging here emphasizing different aspects of collecting vintage items with a generous number of pictures of the classic items under discussion.

3. The marketing angle astutely yet tastefully presented by these active links will take visitors to the Retro Attic eBay Store and companion eCrater shopping site.

4. And, as noted in Chapter 8, Retro Attic has been very choosy about which friends it accepts into its eclectic fold and which will gain Top Friend display. Notice how every one of these Top Friends features similarly styled vintage imagery, further supporting the mood and intent of the Retro Attic page.

Sometimes kitschy but always classy, the Retro Attic page practically compels you to mix up a martini or a Manhattan as you soak up the retro style here. This serves as an excellent example of a companion page intent upon sharing information about the passion for vintage items, never pushing any sort of hard sell but making links to the Retro Attic offerings always easily within reach.

17

CASE STUDY:
WETA
COLLECTIBLES

C alling all fantasy collectors. The next time you're near Wellington, New Zealand, be sure to drop in on an alternate dimension known as the Weta Workshop. If such a trip isn't on your current itinerary, then navigate over to www.myspace.com/wetacollectibles to get a virtual tour of the strange worlds and even stranger inhabitants of the Weta realm.

WHAT IS WETA COLLECTIBLES?

Although you might not have heard about New Zealand's Weta Workshop and are as yet unfamiliar with what goes on there, chances are you're very aware of the work it produces. It's simply the four-time Academy Award winners responsible for the incredible designs and effects seen in *The Lord of the Rings* trilogy and the 2005 reimagining of *King Kong*.

When fantasy fans beheld the incredible works of this talented team from down, down under, the cry went out for souvenirs, and Weta responded with its always growing line of museum quality sculptures and artwork that can grace any film fan's favorite den or other such space. And although Weta enjoyed a very impressive Web presence through its well-designed site, www.wetanz.com/ collectibles, it shrewdly created a promotional MySpace page that helped extend the message that all things from other worlds could be found at Weta.

SIZING UP THE WETA COLLECTIBLES PAGE

You know you've crossed over into a different plane when you explore the Weta Collectibles page. It's clean, clever, and completely entertaining without being overwhelming or overburdened with slow-to-load content. In fact, it loads very quickly and gives you a near-immediate look at the wild wares the Weta team has to share. Most notably, the page succeeds in these areas (as called out in Figure 17.1):

1. The intent of this MySpace page is made clear as the Weta team has established an updated default image that heralds the big news of a major "reveal" that's coming soon. This

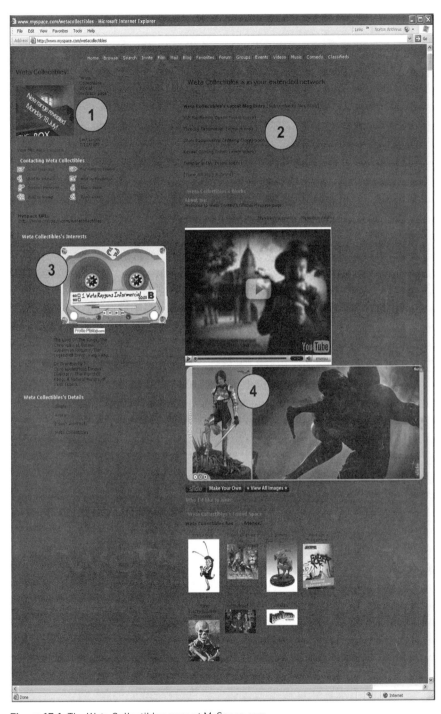

Figure 17.1 The Weta Collectibles page at MySpace.com.

immediately lets fans know that a new line of collectibles is on the way and that the Weta page is one to keep an eye on in the weeks and months to come.

2. The blogging here is reflective of the same material being published on the Weta Collectibles main site, ensuring that their bases are well covered when it comes to letting as many folks as possible, worldwide, know about what's going on at Weta.

3. The embedded audio content features a whimsical cassette tape graphic that plays an entertaining infomercial about Weta's featured collectible.

4. Last, a compelling slideshow reveals many of the excellent collectible items available to buy at Weta Collectibles.

The Weta Collectibles page is a very professional endeavor, yet the people who created it know better than to overwhelm visitors with too much technical trickery. The focus of the page is the work of the Weta team and the collectibles that fans can purchase for themselves. This page is conspicuous in the way it features the slideshow of new Weta products, urging visitors to visit the official Weta site to purchase or preorder, as well as plainly promote the Weta team's next whereabouts on the trade show and convention circuit. And, given there's always something new crawling out of the workshop, this Weta Collectibles page is continually updated to ensure that you're bound to discover something new each time you visit.

18

CASE STUDY:
DARK HORSE COMICS

I f it's comics you want, then Dark Horse Comics has the graphic entertainment you seek. Not your mainstream comic publisher, per se, Dark Horse Comics presents edgy content that will tweak your adrenals, for sure. The MySpace page is an interesting place to visit to learn more about the organization and its vast line of comic series. Find it at www.myspace.com/darkhorsecomics.

WHAT IS DARK HORSE COMICS?

The name "Dark Horse" wasn't selected accidentally. Founder Mike Richardson was determined to go up against the mighty mavens of Marvel and DC Comics with his own independent publishing company. Already successful with his chain of retail comic stores, Richardson was nonetheless dissatisfied with much of the product that he sold and sought something with greater style and sensibility that he believed the industry could produce. Rather than wait for someone else to do something about it, he threw caution to the wind and invested his retail store profits in his upstart entry, Dark Horse Comics.

Established in 1986, his publishing company quickly found an appreciative audience and lured industry talent to develop some truly captivating graphic experiences including *Aliens*, *Hellboy*, and *Sin City*. But Dark Horse is not simply a counterculture endeavor; it has also proved itself to be equally competent in producing entertaining works based upon licensed material including Peter Jackson's *King Kong*, *Star Wars*, and *The Incredibles*.

SIZING UP THE DARK HORSE COMICS PAGE

Working as a satellite to its main site (www.darkhorse.com), the Dark Horse Comics MySpace page is alive with hot-off-the-press information and announcements about new Dark Horse releases and industry events where the Dark Horse team will be appearing to meet and greet its fans (and ideally sell some comics in the process). This particular page is highly engaging thanks to these key elements (as called out in Figure 18.1):

1. The astounding background image shows off the kind of impeccable artwork that fans have come to expect from

Figure 18.1 The Dark Horse Comics page at MySpace.com.

Dark Horse. Newcomers to the publisher's work will immediately see that these people are no amateurs.

2. The blogging here is so fresh that the ink's practically still wet. On this particular visit, I learned more about the Dark Horse appearance planned for the upcoming San Diego ComicCon, which is a contest. What do you get if you win? You join filmmaker Joss Whedon for dinner and get exclusive previews of new comics rolling off the press.

3. Since Dark Horse is well known for many of its ongoing comic series, the team has offered easy-to-download computer desktop backgrounds so fans can enjoy the Dark Horse images every time they boot up.

4. For those new to the Dark Horse experience, there's a comprehensive list of all of the Dark Horse Comics series with accompanying cover art.

The Dark Horse Comics page at MySpace embodies the same sense of off-the-beaten-path presentation that inspired founder Richardson two decades ago and has made his products highly sought-after by enthusiasts and collectors. Knowing that its audience is always looking for more ways to learn more about favorite characters and series, this MySpace page proves to be very well designed to deftly market the company and its products. It's definitely worth looking over, especially as an example of how modern-day marketing can perfectly coexist with offbeat but alluring content.

CASE STUDY:
ERICA GABRIELLE
STUDIO

Now that we've spent some time at a couple of larger-scale company pages, let's return to an individual's page that works admirably well to promote an artist and her work. If its evocative and emotive photography that inspires you, pay a visit to Erica Gabrielle's page at www.myspace.com/ericagabriellestudio.

WHO IS ERICA GABRIELLE?

Erica Gabrielle is a multimedia artist, applying her unique perspective to the mediums of photography and film. A 2001 graduate of New York's School of Visual Arts, Erica has quickly demonstrated her knack for capturing alluring and evocative images through the eye of her camera. She currently specializes in portraiture, and one look at her Friends' comments will tell you that she comes highly recommended and is highly respected.

SIZING UP THE ERICA GABRIELLE STUDIO PAGE

Working as a companion to her main Web site (www.ericagabrielle studio.com), Ms. Gabrielle has leveraged the MySpace experience in a way that gains her increased exposure yet doesn't distract her away from her livelihood. This page is not the most elegant or intrinsically designed, but it doesn't need to be. Clearly, this is a *signpost* page that does the job it's intended to do: to spread the word about her work and redirect visitors to her main Web site. While I might suggest that that Ms. Gabrielle add more content to this page (especially a slideshow that would feature her wonderful work), this design succeeds nonetheless thanks to the following elements (as called out in Figure 19.1):

1. Here's another fine example of the power of a compelling default photo, this one immediately showing Ms. Gabrielle's unique eye for capturing a mood within her photographic composition.

2. The link to Ms. Gabrielle's official Web site is easily found and deserves to be visited.

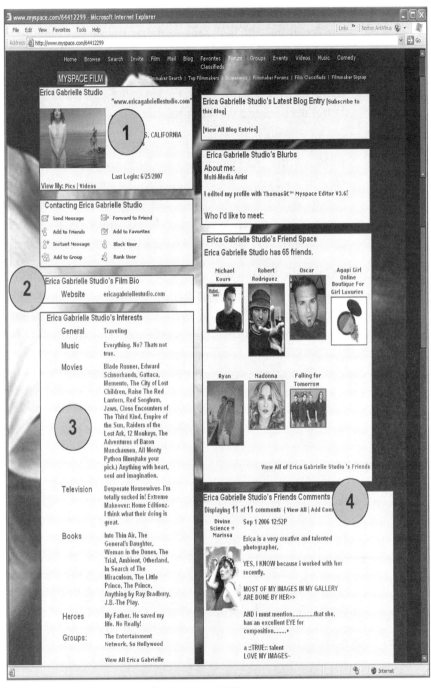

Figure 19.1 The Erica Gabrielle Studio page at MySpace.com.

3. Ms. Gabrielle wisely provides plenty of information regarding her interests, likely recognizing the need for a photographic artist to bond personally with each and every one of her clients. This list of interests lets prospective subjects learn more about the artist's personal likes and style to better accelerate a working relationship.

4. When it comes to art and photography, the beauty is definitely within the eye of the beholder, and it takes word of mouth to assure others that this artist can deliver the goods. To that end, Ms. Gabrielle keeps her Friends Comments section easily visible with testimony regarding the satisfaction that people have found with her work and style.

Erica Gabrielle is a talented and artistic photographer and one who recognizes the value of getting seen wherever and whenever possible. Her page works as a virtual business card with just enough information to attract potential clients who are looking for compelling photography to polish up their personal portfolios. To that end, this MySpace page works quite well to help others learn about what Ms. Gabrielle can do for them.

CASE STUDY:
GIRL SCOUT COOKIES

For our last stop, how about a bit of dessert to top off this multi-course experience? When you're looking for something to satisfy your sweet tooth and ease your craving for something munchy, why not reach for a box of the renowned favorites brought to you by those little darlings dressed in green and brown. I'm talking about Girl Scout cookies, of course, and you'll find they, too, have a MySpace page at www.myspace.com/girlscoutcookiesale.

WHAT IS THE GIRL SCOUT
COOKIE SALE?

Girl Scout cookies hardly need introduction since any of us who have worked in offices or wandered past the well-stocked tables at a supermarket entrance have seen the boxes of tempting treats presented by those infectiously energetic young girls. Girl Scout cookie sales practically command their own annual season and always result in cases upon cases sold to help the Girl Scouts of the USA raise funds.

Interestingly enough, most folks think that once "cookie season" is over, the treats disappear until next year's round. The fact is that a quick visit to the official Web site, www.girlscoutcookies.org, shows that these treats are available year round, usually within your own local area. However, that may not be common enough knowledge, so the Girl Scouts organization has established this MySpace page to help tell even more folks that their favorite Thin Mints, Tagalongs, and chewy Samoas are still obtainable.

SIZING UP THE GIRL SCOUT
COOKIE SALE PAGE

Working as an extension of the main Web presence, the Girl Scout Cookie Sale page is as fun and lively as the colorful boxes of treats it promotes. But this particular page design also makes the most of the community aspect of MySpace, working to explain more about the organization beyond its tasty snacks. Specifically, here are the points of interest of this page (as called out in Figure 20.1):

1. Astutely situated along the top of the page is a custom set of active links that helps visitors immediately find out

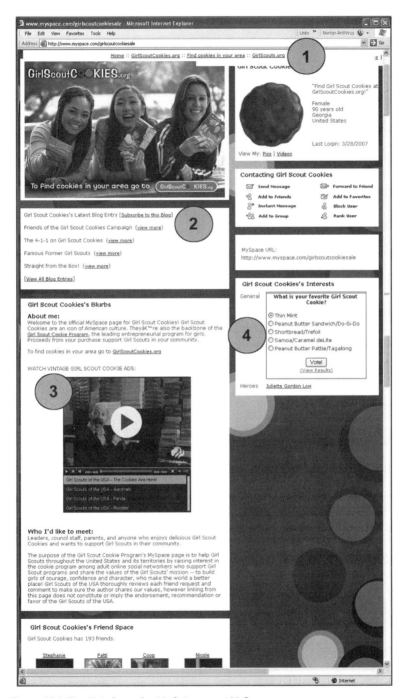

Figure 20.1 The Girls Scout Cookie Sale page at MySpace.com.

how to get cookies in their area or learn more about the organization itself.

2. Fun blog entries tell more about the cookie crusade and even share information about former scouts who went on to become famous.

3. For the nostalgic among us who have enjoyed Girl Scout cookies for decades, here's a fun bit of video content that reveals a vintage cookie commercial.

4. Last, this fun survey lets you vote for your favorite cookie and view the results to see how your view stacks up against the votes of other visitors.

All in all, the Girl Scout Cookie Sale page is fun and engaging. It strikes a perfect balance between the delectable sweets and the organization behind them. Now that you know about it, why not pay this page a visit because wouldn't some nicely chilled Thin Mints make a perfect after-dinner treat?

MORE **IDEAS**
FOR MARKETING
YOUR **SPACE**

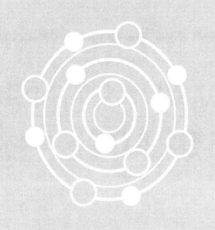

KEEPING YOUR **FRIENDS** COMING BACK

Success at MySpace can be summed up in a single word—*participation*. In order to reap the most of the MySpace experience for your money-making endeavors, you have to be involved consistently and, to the best of your ability, constantly. Think about it: The Web sites you probably visit the most are the ones that maintain a constant flow of new material and updates to existing content. Whether you're online shopping for goods, services, or information, there's little reason to return to a

portal that never changes. At MySpace, the same principle applies—
update it or forget it.

This chapter takes a look at several ways you can keep your
MySpace page fresh and inviting without having it take over your
time entirely. There's a happy medium to be struck when managing your MySpace page, and this chapter has what you need to keep
your friends coming back to your page.

UPDATING YOUR PAGE DESIGN WITHOUT MOUNTING TOTAL REDESIGN

Keeping your page fresh and compelling means that you'll want to
"rotate the stock," so to speak. In other words, you'll want to alter
certain aspects of your page design, if for no other reason, to let
folks know you're cognizant of the ever-changing and evolving
world around you, online and within the real world. But you
shouldn't be concerned that this means that you'll be forever
redesigning you page; far from it. Instead, make preparations
to modify these key elements of your page, all of which can be
managed in as little as a few hours of any given week:

- *Update your default image.* Although you need to remember that, when you change your default image, it will also
  change at all of your current friends' pages (so be tasteful).
  It's a good idea to update this image if your business can
  benefit from it. Recall the example of Weta Collectibles and
  how that page uses the default image to serve as a highly
  visible banner for an upcoming product release. And
  although you would normally not change away from your
  product or company brand (such as DVD Verdict), you can
  add seasonal adornments to the image just to keep things
  fun and interesting.

- *Change your background color or image.* Again, if you've established a company design and color scheme, you might not need to make a change here, but you should see whether, like the default image, you can make appropriate changes throughout the year without diluting your brand. Recalling the Dark Horse Comics example, it would be a good idea that the background image there be changed to reflect a new comic release or a promotional spotlight on a particular artist or contributor, and if you look at Figure 21.1, you'll see that Dark Horse Comics did just that.

- *Change any selected audio or video content.* Just as you need to mind and manage your friends to see if their

Figure 21.1 To keep its page fresh, Dark Horse Comics has modified its background *and* default image to reflect a new comic being promoted.

default images have changed in a way that doesn't suit your page or your patrons, you also need to keep track of the embedded audio and video content on your page. Since these are merely links to content hosted elsewhere on MySpace or an external site, sometimes those links go dead. For example, if the Cheap Trick page removed "I Want You to Want Me" from its jukebox, the link from my page would cease to function and would indicate that the link is dead; it's time to update it.

Besides this general maintenance stuff, consider adding new content from time to time by way of blogs, additional profile customizations, and so on. You needn't go to the effort of completely resetting your profile unless that serves a business purpose (*relaunch* and *reinvention* are still hot phrases used by the hypesters). Consider, also, if a partner page launch would work better for you in that you'd establish your main page and then launch spin-off and spoke sites from there (which is my intention with the Dencomm page because it will serve as the hub to additional pages I have in the works at the time of this writing).

TURNING ON THE FEED FROM YOUR MAIN WEB SITE

Although this is certainly an advanced feature, it would be worthwhile for to you to investigate implementing an RSS feed to or from your MySpace page. What's an *RSS feed*? For starters, it's an acronym for "real simple syndication," and it means just what it says—syndication of content for direct broadcast wherever you like. In simplified terms, this means that you can create a stream of information that is fed by content you establish one place on the Internet and is automatically forwarded to other destinations you establish. Essentially, you write it once, and it gets displayed in many other places.

An example of RSS at work on MySpace is the DVD Verdict page. Notice in Figure 21.2 that the block that contains the most recent DVD reviews posted on the site is actually fed on this page by an RSS feed. The team at DVD Verdict created this feed from its own page to keep this MySpace page updated every time new reviews are posted on their main site (and at DVD Verdict, this is done *daily*). Talk about fresh content.

If your next question is, "How do I create an RSS feed for my page?" that's a question that can't be answered within the scope of this discussion. But, not to leave you high and dry, I would recommend your reading *Developing Feeds with RSS and Atom* by Ben Hammersley. Additionally, there's a great online workshop hosted by the State of Utah Online Services that's completely free.

The intention of this brief introduction to RSS is not to derail the point of this chapter but, rather support it while furthering the assertion that keeping your page compelling doesn't have to require that you remain chained to your computer. Fresh information on your page is important to keeping visitors returning but you also have a business to run and employing a tool like RSS can be a true time saver and is almost like hiring another person to do the time-consuming work for you.

Figure 21.2 The faint RSS icon indicates that the content on this part of the DVD Verdict MySpace page is being automatically fed by an RSS feed.

SELL YOUR BRAND FIRST AND YOUR PRODUCTS SECOND

A key principle to understand and embody in managing a business-supportive MySpace page is to reduce the pitch when speaking to Spacers. At MySpace, the community is particularly sensitive to the notion that marketers will overrun the place, turning it into one big commercial full of never-ending spam advertising. However, the demographic analysis is still the most accurate indicator for who's using MySpace (refer back to Figure 1.4). Given those statistics, the site isn't anywhere near dead as some younger folks might contend (they just get bored easily, don't they?). Nevertheless, take heed that you don't fulfill that dire prophecy; refrain from unbounded pitching within the MySpace realm. On your page, try to emphasize the following as they relate to you, your brand, and your offering:

- *Reach out to your target audience first.* Theoretically, your product or service was developed with a demographic in mind, so lean your communications toward that group. Speak to these people directly in your tone, style, and content to secure their attention before trying to conquer the world. Your brand stands a much better chance of becoming established if you tailor it to one segment first and then see if it makes sense to widen it to an extended audience.

- *Communicate with your target audience as much as possible.* You can do this in direct dialogue (messages, comments, maybe even Instant Messaging if you decide to enable that) to build relationships. When you build relationships, you build trust, and those to whom you reach out will be more likely to try your wares and tell their friends about them too.

- *Keep your page active with content—music, video, blog matter—that is relevant to your target audience.* Again, you're angling your brand to a target group, and you need to win the attention and approval of the people in the group if your brand is going to succeed. The products or services tied to the brand will naturally become visible to the members of your audience *after* they've come to know, like, and trust your brand.

- *Keep your page simple and fast-loading.* Your audience—*any* audience, for that matter—hasn't much patience for a slow-loading page, and you'll likely hurt your brand if it becomes associated with snail-paced performance.

Keep your audience in sight, and lean your brand its way. Talk about the relevant sorts of things that the audience enjoys *besides your products.* As much as you don't want to turn your page into an "about me" endeavor, you still need to make it more personal than an e-commerce Web site. This is the difference—and opportunity—of adding a MySpace page to your business plan. Bottom line: Make your page like the old *Cheers* television comedy—where everyone knows your name.

LET YOUR VISITORS BE YOUR GUIDE

After you've focused on your brand, put on some listening ears to hear what your visitors (hopefully soon-to-be "customers") have to tell you. One of the worst mistakes any businessperson can make is to adopt the self-centered attitude that goes, "My customers love all of my products—just ask me." Customers will tell you what they like and don't like; what they want and don't want. If you'll listen attentively to them, they'll give you the answers that will lead to success as they freely guide you down the path of sales, sales, and more sales. Don't pitch, just listen.

So how do you put on your listening ears? Simple. Open your MySpace page to input and feedback from your friends. Here's where you're harnessing the natural rhythm and intent of MySpace—to interact with others. When you adopt MySpace to further a brand and a business, the key to better results is to add *interactivity* to your page. The best news is that interactivity is easy:

- *Allow your friends to post comments to your page.* Remember that you can elect to approve all comments before they're posted (and that's how I like to manage things in the beginning), but you can also allow comments to be posted without approval. Either way, let your friends post comments and see that their words are on display. This gives them a feeling that they're visible on your page as well as on their own (a key to increasing exposure, personally or professionally) but also that you're an engaging sort of person who hasn't nipped the MySpace experience in the bud before it could ever blossom.

- *Post blogs and allow "Kudos & comments" to them.* Since the intent of a blog is to share ideas and opinions or solicit feedback, leave the "disable Kudos & comments" box unchecked (see Figure 21.3). If you intend to share engaging information and perspectives—and you should—then

Figure 21.3 Uncheck the box and improve the participation levels at your page when you post blog entries.

let your friends engage you in discussion. Recall that you can restrict the visibility of your blog entries to only your friends or a segregated population thereof but, if you can, try to open the blog visibility to the entire MySpace community in order for others to see the discussion and possibly entice them to become a friend to you and your brand.

- *Take a poll.* Most people will speak right up when asked to give their opinion or "vote for their favorite." You can engage your friends and visitors immediately when you provide a fun or fact-finding poll on you MySpace page. There are some great tools out there that will build a nifty radio-button-controlled poll such as AcePolls (www.acepolls.com), easily and for free (you just include links that provide navigation back to the site. There are other poll tools, too, so search your favorite portal for "MySpace polls" to find others. You can see an example of a fun and fast poll I created for my page in Figure 21.4.

CONSIDER SHARING CONTENT TO INCREASE VISIBILITY

Another way to keep your friends coming back to your page is to provide content that you didn't create. Although we're not all recording artists, we can still embed music files on our pages, right? And, even though few of us are filmmakers or videographers, we can all include streaming video content on our pages. This same principle holds for information and active links that might lead to other pages, other Web sites, or other blogs where the information is of interest to you and might also be of interest

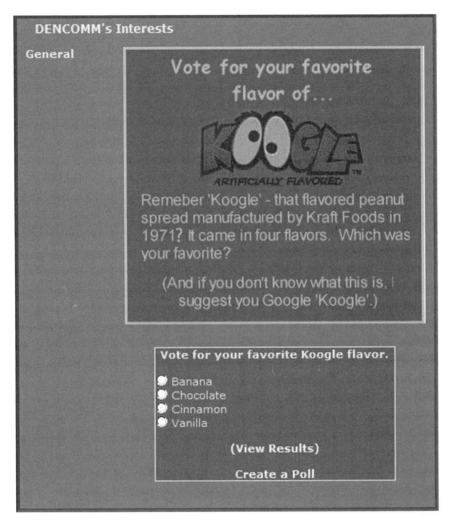

Figure 21.4 Polls like this one are easy to create and fun for your friends and visitors to participate in.

to your friends and visitors. If you're good at ferreting out the sort of "gems of knowledge" that others watch for, include that information on your page, and it will likely add up to another compelling feature of your MySpace presence—all you have to do is link to it.

CONTINUE TO CHOOSE
YOUR FRIENDS WISELY

A final point to consider in your MySpace experience is to remember to keep a close eye on your friends lists so the people you call "pals" aren't the sort that are likely to discourage others from striking up a relationship with you. You don't want to be snobbish or prudish as you hand-pick your friends, but you don't want to appear as though you're a newbie who is either (1) too green to realize many MySpace "friends" are just bogus accounts or (2) so eager to tally up a high friend count that you'll appear lacking in your integrity (something that will tarnish your brand in your audience's eyes). Keep a close watch on whom you accept as friends, reviewing their profiles before you accept (or deny) them and then monitoring their default images as they appear within your MySpace page. If you feel the need to quickly boost a friend count (and some Spacers believe that a high count is necessary for attracting more friends), then definitely maintain your Top Friends to include only visible links that fit within the style and intent of your page and your brand.

MySpace Tip

One parting suggestion: When you correspond on behalf of your brand or your business activities, be sure that you include reference to your MySpace page. Don't be bashful about this; all the major brands and corporations are doing this, and it's paying off by way of increased visibility and interaction with you, your page, and your brand.

SPIN-OFF
SPACES

By now, you've seen mention and use of several other Web sites brimming with tools to help you improve your MySpace experience and give your page that custom, cool, and commercially attractive touch. Much like the eBay phenomenon of the 1990s, MySpace has emerged as a thriving endeavor that has spawned a virtual cottage industry, just as when auction mania hit. If you search for MySpace-related sites from your favorite portal—Yahoo!, Google, or wherever—you'll be overwhelmed by a multitude of search hits that lead you to a seemingly endless list of Web destinations eager to help you sharpen your space.

Some are less helpful than others, and many are just downright useless—fronts for unabashed affiliate links and unapologetic pop-ups by the score. Even so, there *are* some sites that are helpful and very useful in developing and delivering your MySpace presence. Throughout this book I've mentioned many but here are a few more of the better sites I've encountered that you might want to visit.

MySPACE EDITOR
(www.myspaceeditor.org)

MySpace Editor is called "the simplest MySpace editor around," and it's true. The layout of this profile editing tool (see Figure 22.1) is visually lackluster but it enables you to easily create a stylish MySpace profile of your own without having to fend off animations, pop-ups, and obnoxious adware (you will encounter just a couple of nonintrusive Google ads).

ACE POLLS (www.AcePolls.com)

I mentioned this in Chapter 21 but never said much about it. There are plenty of online portals that will help you create polls for your MySpace page, but Ace Polls seems to be the best among them (see Figure 22.2). Creating the poll is quick and simple thanks to a WYSIWYG (what-you-see-is-what-you-get) design that shows what your poll will look like as you create it. Plenty of color options

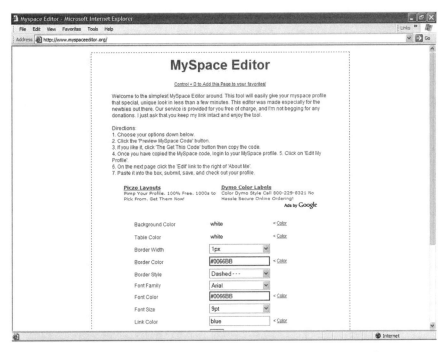

Figure 22.1 No frills gets you a whole lot of fancy when you customize your MySpace profile using MySpace Editor.

are available to create a poll that works within the scheme of your MySpace page.

TOOLS FOR MySPACE
(www.toolsformyspace.com)

Tools for MySpace is a bit too busy with affiliate ads and sponsored links, but it still delivers some great tools to help you create unique touches for your MySpace page (see Figure 22.3). Navigate the page carefully, and you'll find a really fun image editor—TFMS Image Editor—among other tools like a scroll box designer, a contact table designer, and other fun stuff.

Figure 22.2 Creating polls for your MySpace is easy and fun when you use Ace Polls.

Figure 22.3 Although it emphasizes its contributions to MySpace profile editing, the Tools for MySpace site has some fun other tools that are worth checking out.

PYZAM (www.pyzam.com)

Formerly known as FreeFlashToys.com, Pyzam is full of all sorts of blingy thingies that could choke your MySpace page and gag your guests, but it has some really fun virtual toys that you might enjoy. I smiled when I saw the lava lamp, the Magic 8-Ball, and the PONG game. Click on the *Toys* box (or the left-column navigation selection, *Flash Toys*) from the home page (see Figure 22.4) and play with and pick some of the fun items. The code for each is provided for free for an immediate cut and paste into your MySpace profile (just be aware that you'll be actively advertising for Pyzam, but so what?).

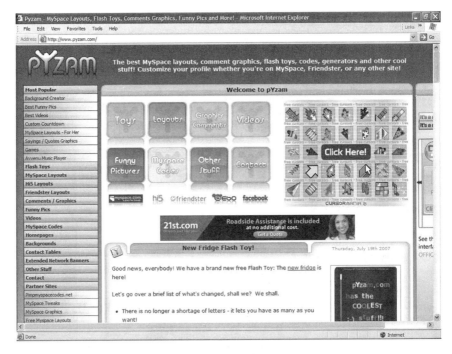

Figure 22.4 Pyzam has some fun toys and other stuff that you can easily add to your MySpace page. Just don't overdo it.

FREE WEB LAYOUTS
(www.freeweblayouts.com)

Finally, if all these fun goodies sound great but your still struggling with how to create an overall themed layout for yourself, click on over to FreeWebLayouts.com where you can choose from among a near plethora of designs to get you on your way (see Figure 22.5). As the name suggests, it's all free.

So just like any other new tool that can be used for meeting and marketing, the MySpace phenomenon has given rise to a host of helpers—individuals, small companies, and the "widgets" they offer up—to take some of the difficulty out of creating a truly compelling presentation. Sample the sites mentioned here to make your MySpace customizing a fun and fruitful endeavor.

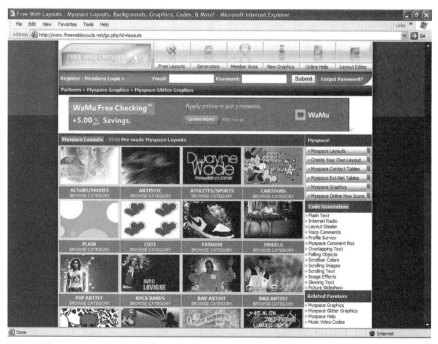

Figure 22.5 If you have "designer's block," don't fret. Just get over to FreeWebLayouts.com to break the ice and select from the many ready-to-apply designs.

OTHER **SPACES** FOR MORE **FACES**

For a final stop on this journey into the world of MySpace, your business, and the additional opportunities available to help you make money and embolden your brand, here are a few more sites you might want to visit. Each of these embodies the social networking spirit and can be excellent additional avenues for your business prosperity. Some, however, can be fun personal sites where you can loosen your collar, kick your shoes off, and enjoy some downtime with others.

Classmates.com
(www.classmates.com)

You may recall from Chapter 1 that this is the site that started the social networking phenomenon we enjoy today (see Figure 23.1). Although this site is mentioned in that chapter for historical reference in this context, it's worth noting that it's also an interesting place to register and participate in because you'll be amazed at how many of your former classmates—buddies, beauties, and bullies—are already there. This is a great way to catch up with your former peers to find out "whatever happened to" whomever while also determining whether there's some worthwhile networking to harness. And they probably won't recognize you now that you've ditched the horn-rimmed glasses and shed the wire braces.

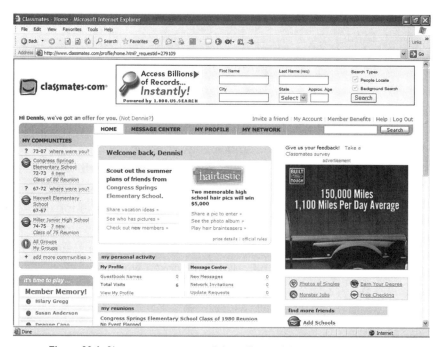

Figure 23.1 Classmates.com started the online social networking industry.

Figure 23.2 At LinkedIn, the topics are not necessarily all work, but they're certainly not just about play.

LinkedIn.com (www.linkedin.com)

LinkedIn is a social networking site built with a business mindset. Perhaps a friend or associate sent to you an invitation to join his or her LinkedIn network of associates; if you didn't know what that meant, you could register at LinkedIn to learn where many of the business-minded folks have been congregating to share ideas, opportunities, and inspiration to others just like them (see Figure 23.2).

Facebook.com (www.facebook.com)

Facebook is social networking site that originally began as a private conclave for the students of Harvard University. The population soon began to include members of surrounding Boston-area

Figure 23.3 Despite this rather uninspired welcome page for newcomers, Facebook is the new online hangout for the younger set.

colleges and now is home to the collegiate crowd from across the nation and around the world. It started allowing members to invite high school–aged friends, and now it's wide open to all Internet users, with a 30-million-plus user base, making it one of the hottest of the social networking sites. If you want to keep track of what the younger crowd likes, dislikes, and spends money on, log in and listen at Facebook (see Figure 23.3).

FRIENDSTER (www.friendster.com)

Another site, Friendster, is popular among a younger demographic (ages 18–30). It is another space to keep an eye on if you're tracking trends in this age group (see Figure 23.4). As an interesting side

Figure 23.4 Friendster is another site to check out if you're tracking youth culture.

note, reported statistics reveal that Friendster is largely populated with users from the Philippines and Malaysia, important to know if you want or need to network with folks from these regions or if you think that they are a strong audience for your products or services.

XANGA (www.xanga.com)

Next, there's Xanga, which sort of sounds like a tabletop party game for the moderately intoxicated adult, but it's actually a site founded in 1998 that leveraged the rising popularity of blogging. At Xanga, you can register to get a site of your own (similar to MySpace) with tools to create and manage Weblogs, photoblogs, videoblogs, and audioblogs. Most often, the Xanga members use the site as a personal journal of sorts, and it can serve that purpose

Figure 23.5 Speak your mind in word, photo, video, and audio at Xanga; it might be the break from business that you're looking for.

well if you're looking for an outlet for your innermost thoughts and are unafraid to share those with others. See Figure 23.5.

GATHER (www.gather.com)

Finally, if ever there was a site serving as the virtual "water cooler" for timely discussion, it's Gather.com. Just as you'd seek out a friend, coworker, or family member to discuss the latest political situation, good movie, or compelling novel, folks who congregate at Gather are chatting about the same things. The opinions are wide and varied, and the site maintains civil decorum. Even if you don't have much to say yourself, you'll quickly see that just reading along makes for a scintillating experience where you can truly find out what's on other people's minds.

Although the above thumbnail peeks at these other social networking sites haven't focused specifically on the business opportunity of each of these additional online meeting places, understand that each has the same potential as MySpace to provide yet another platform for you to promote your fine offerings. Each site has slight differences but each can be harnessed to do what you came for— to spread the word around thriving online communities about what it is you and your business can supply. Enjoy!

CHECKLIST
TO
SUCCESS

Much has been covered in the previous 23 chapters, and it's likely that you're looking to distill it all down now into an easy-to-apply list of steps for creating, maintaining, and promoting your MySpace presence. Good news. You'll find that list below. Following are the steps you need to take to implement the approach for harnessing MySpace for your business success. If you want to re-review the details of each item presented, use the chapter references to refresh your understanding.

Best of luck and best of business to you at MySpace.

MAKING MONEY WITH MySPACE: CHECKLIST

1. Develop a plan (Chapters 1 and 2).

   - Establish the purpose of your MySpace page (in relation to your existing business place or Web presence).

   - Define the target audience you seek to attract.

   - Choose a method for engaging your audience (e.g., links, blogs, product release updates, upcoming events, etc.).

   - Decide on the timing of your MySpace launch.

2. Sketch out a design (Chapter 3).

   - Research other similar MySpace pages to determine how you'll fit in or stand out.

   - Determine the look and feel you'll seek to establish within your page.

   - Determine whether you have the capabilities to develop a complex site (if a complex site is what you need).

   - Determine how much time you can and will devote to maintaining and updating your page.

   - Acquire the help (persons, tools) you'll need to develop the site you have in mind.

3. Register at MySpace (Chapters 4 and 5).

   - Enter basic information.

   - Establish a relevant and easy-to-remember and easy-to-type MySpace URL.

- Establish your privacy and security settings.

- Mark your page as *private* while you work on the design.

4. Customize your page (Chapters 6 and 7).

  - Use MySpace basic profile editor, MySpace advanced profile editor, or third-party profile generators.

  - Add video and audio elements.

  - Test the results.

  - Verify the load time.

5. Launch your page (Chapters 8, 9, and 10).

  - Set your page to "public."

  - Begin sending friend requests to relevant page owners.

  - Respond to friend requests you receive.

  - Monitor default photos of your friends (remove friend if photo is objectionable or runs counter to the message you're trying to convey through your page).

  - Begin blurb updates and launch your blog.

6. Establish your page maintenance schedule (Chapter 21).

  - Update your default image as needed (e.g., season changes, business conditions, etc.).

  - Modify your page's background as needed.

  - Ensure that audio and video content remains playable and relevant.

  - Establish feeds (e.g., RSS) from a main business Web site or blog site you may have.

  - Maintain your message to properly target your audience.

- Pay attention to feedback and make adjustments to your page and message as appropriate.

Keep this checklist handy when you begin your MySpace setup and as you work to keep you page lively and compelling. Refer to the chapters referenced for further details of each step.

APPENDIX:
ADDITIONAL REFERENCES AND RESOURCES

In this book, I make reference to a few additional resources that will answer many of your questions about money and marketing matters, both online and offline. Although this list of resources isn't the most exhaustive you'll find, I've found these to be some of the *best* resources I've spent time with, and I think you will find them helpful too.

WEB RESOURCES

http://www.everythingtech.tv/2006/05/24/disable-myspace-css/.

Visit everythingTech to access this article, which provides video content showing how to disable CSS code from some particularly overdone MySpace pages.

http://rssgov.com/rssworkshop.html.

Here's a useful online workshop hosted by the State of Utah Online Services division. It has the right information to show you how RSS feeds are created and maintained. And, best of all, this instruction is *free.*

BOOKS

Gladwell, Malcolm, *The Tipping Point: How Little Things Can Make a Big Difference* (Back Bay Books, 2002).

Hammersley, Ben, *Developing Feeds with RSS and Atom* (California: O'Reilly Media, Inc., 2005).

Lindstrom, Martin, *BRAND Sense: Build Powerful Brands through Touch, Taste, Smell, Sight and Sound* (New York: Free Press, 2005).

Underhill, Paco, *Why We Buy: The Science of Shopping* (New York: Simon and Schuster, 2000).

INDEX

Dennis L. Prince is a well-recognized and long-trusted advocate for online auction-goers. He continues his tireless efforts to instruct, enlighten, and enable auction enthusiasts and business owners, assuring his readers' success every step of the way. His perpetual passion for online auctioning and adherence to good business practices has earned him recognition as one of the Top Ten Online Auction Movers and Shakers by Vendio.com (formerly AuctionWatch.com). His insight and perspectives are regularly sought by others covering the online auction industry. He has been featured in the nationally distributed *Entrepreneur Magazine* (2003) and *Access Magazine* (2000). And he has been a guest of highly rated television and radio programs such as TechTV, BBC-Radio, and C/Net Radio.

Besides his previous books about eBay and Internet commerce, his vast editorial contributions to industry stalwarts like Vendio.com (formerly AuctionWatch), Krause Publications, Collector Online, and Auctiva have earned him a well-regarded reputation in his ongoing analysis of the online auction industry. He likewise maintains active interaction with his ever-expanding personal network of auction enthusiasts, power sellers, and passionate collectors, both online and offline.